YO-BUC-819

GORDON I. SHEA

Managing a difficult or hostile audience

WITHDRAWN

A SPECTRUM BOOK

Prentice-Hall, Inc., Englewood Cliffs, New Jersey 07632

SAN BRUNO PUBLIC LIBRARY, SAN BRUNO, CALIF.

Library of Congress Cataloging in Publication Data

SHEA, GORDON F.
  Managing a difficult or hostile audience.
  "A Spectrum Book."
  Includes index.
  1. Public speaking. 2. Meetings. 3. Audiences.
I. Title.
PN4121.S38 1984   808.5′1   84-11537
ISBN 0-13-550674-3
ISBN 0-13-550666-2 (pbk.)

658.45
S

© 1984 by Prentice-Hall, Inc., Englewood Cliffs, New Jersey 07632

All rights reserved. No part of this book
may be reproduced in any form or by any means
without permission in writing from the publisher.

10 9 8 7 6 5 4 3 2 1

Printed in the United States of America.

Editorial/production supervision by Claudia Citarella
Manufacturing buyer: Pat Mahoney
Cover designer: Hal Siegel

A SPECTRUM BOOK

ISBN 0-13-550666-2 {PBK.}

ISBN 0-13-550674-3

This book is available at a special discount when ordered
in bulk quantities. Contact Prentice-Hall, Inc.,
General Publishing Division, Special Sales,
Englewood Cliffs, New Jersey 07632.

To *Joellyn M. Shea*, who is a delight to my life

Contents

Preface

This is *not* a book on public speaking although it contains many ideas that can help you to make a first-class speech or presentation. This is *not* a book on how to conduct meetings, although it offers much on how to plan, organize, and run successful meetings. However, this *is* a book on how to work productively with audiences and groups when hostility, fear, apathy, boredom, or defeatism shadow the proceedings.

This is a practitioner's handbook. It is mostly organized from the viewpoint of the speaker, presenter, meeting planner, moderator, panel participant, group spokesperson, or group leader. It can be used by anyone who has a hand in the conduct of a meeting.

This book aims at providing practical ideas and techniques. The reading is purposely not slowed by voluminous references and distracting footnotes. A brief bibliography of basic source material is provided as a starting point for those who wish to read more deeply about the echniques discussed here.

My underlying thesis is that we often waste the time, energy, experience, expertise, and creative thought of ourselves and our audience when we allow negative feelings and thoughts to flow between us unresolved. I hope that by using the techniques described herein we can use these wasted human assets to produce mutually gratifying gains for all of us.

The need for this book became apparent several years ago when I was teaching courses on "How to Make Effective Briefings and Presentations" at the University of Maryland and for private firms and government agencies. In problem solving sessions with course participants it became clear that a great deal of their anxiety about appearing before *any* group was based on the *possibility* of encountering a really tough group. Although they acknowledged that a truly different audience was a rare thing, these were often the really *critical* situations that would greatly affect their job success, their future well-being or their sense of self and peace of mind. Few seemed to realize that there were any general principles or specific skills that they could master and apply in such situations except for experience and common sense.

Although I had no quarrel with experience and common sense, getting the experience is often very costly in critical situations and common sense can often be augmented by know-how and skills gained from research and a study of other people's art. At that point I began to assemble a program specifically designed to equip speakers, presenters, and others who must deal with difficult individuals or groups, with the skills and knowledge they needed to do their job, or gain their objectives in a group setting.

Therefore this book combines a set of proven and reliable public speaking and meeting techniques with a growing set of experientially tested and research-based tools for working well with difficult groups.

In the last decade many hundreds of my course participants from all walks of life have successfully and effectively used these techniques with difficult groups of all sizes and types. During this period I have constantly tested, revised, and improved the techniques offered. This developmental process continues as new findings from the field of communications and the behavioral sciences are tested and incorporated into my courses. The effort to integrate this new material at the current state of the art is what this book is all about.

I appreciate the opportunity offered by the Conferences and Institutes Program at the University of Maryland University College for the continuing opportunity to present, test, and improve my course on "Managing a Difficult or Hostile Audience." This group has included

Arthur Halligan (Executive Director), David Butcher, John DeBerardinis and John Lathrop (Associate Directors), Ann Lano, Jim Yackley, and many others on the staff.

Additional thanks are due to David C. Booker, Yves Savain, David Mitchell, and Professor Donald Kirkley (University of Maryland), who through discussion and review contributed much to this work.

Perhaps the persons who deserve the most credit are Mirga J. Massey, secretary extraordinary, who prepared and edited this manuscript for publication, and Linda Ziedrich, copy editor, who contributed greatly to its clarity and focus.

Lastly I would appreciate your comments and suggestions for the advancement of this important subject. Please write me at the Prime Systems Company, P.O. Box 404, Beltsville, Maryland 20705.

CHAPTER ONE

Keys to managing
a tough audience

Danger and opportunity are the keynotes of our age. Underneath the shadows of potential nuclear war, international terrorism, and economic uncertainty we see the personal lives of average people becoming more diverse and self-directed. Although we see many of our citizens not bothering to vote, we also see people educating themselves, diversifying their skills, and experimenting with new forms of self-governance. While some are opting out of our social systems, more and more are insisting on full and meaningful participation. To paraphrase Dickens—these are the worst of times, these are the best of times.

Nowhere is this paradox more apparent than in the ways we conduct our public and organizational affairs. In the meeting rooms of corporations and governmental agencies, in the halls of unions and clubs, and in our professional societies, and community associations many of our conflicts are getting out of hand.

As a growing proportion of our population becomes indifferent or hostile to authority in general, fewer people are willing to accept impersonal, technical or autocratic decisions about things that affect them. Although more and more bright, articulate, well-educated people are engaging in civic activities, they are often using their talents to block public and private projects rather than to develop and support viable alternatives. To ensure that their complaints are heard, today we frequently find militant special-interest groups trampling on the rights of others. Commonly the work of public agencies at all levels of government is being ground to a standstill by obstructionist tactics. The frequent conflict between those intent on avoiding injury to themselves, and those who are pursuing projects or programs they consider meritorious, is tearing at the fabric of our society.

If the issue at hand is at all controversial, today's public speaker is likely to face an audience that is angry, resisting, fearful or cold—or all of these. To manage one's self well, to conclude a meeting successfully and to avoid negative after-effects challenges all those who are in any way responsible for effecting meeting outcomes.

IS FRUSTRATION OUR FATE?

The question before each of us is: Are there ways to handle deeply divisive emotional issues without our feelings obstructing our common sense and leaving us defeated, ineffective, and resentful? More specifically, for those who have a role to play in our public and private meetings, can we conduct such affairs with speed, competence, and skill, so that the negative tensions in the group are reduced, freeing us to move toward more mutually satisfying conclusions to our meetings? I believe this is possible.

This belief is based on considerable personal experience and on the success of people who have mastered some truly nasty encounters. Basic to this belief are seven conclusions or principles that I've derived from studying such difficult situations. They are as follows:

1 Many long-accepted meeting practices are inadequate for dealing with emotionally negative audiences. Furthermore, many of these methods of conducting meetings are becoming obsolete because they either subtly turn off audience members or cause all the parties involved to settle for less than is necessary.

2 Many new and better meeting techniques are becoming available. Yet widespread public ignorance of them may require you to act in more of a leader–teacher role in sharing these improved ways to get things done in the meetings you conduct or influence.

3 An audience is never uniform nor fixed. Audiences are dynamic and subject to change as are their moods. We can each greatly enhance our skill for constructively influencing their mood without resorting to manipulative tricks or games.

4 There is a wide variety of easily learnable professional methods for planning, organizing, and conducting meetings and making presentations that reduce tension, fear, and anger, and that help you to create more positive moods and results.

5 The adversarial stance we often assume when facing a difficult or resisting group is usually unnecessary and counterproductive.

6 Our personal anxiety and stress can be successfully managed. We can also learn new ways to enhance our personal strength, toughen our self-confidence, and psychologically prepare ourselves to better handle any difficult encounter.

7 If we recognize that our audience is a collection of intelligent, resourceful, and even creative people (even though they are not sympathetic to our needs), we may be able, through collaborative methodologies, to grasp their interest and energy to promote some win–win outcomes from even our most difficult encounters.

In this chapter we will deal with item No. 1: the obsolescence of many of our meeting practices. The other themes are woven through the rest of the book. This is an optimistic book because I've seen its principles work. Frustration need not be our fate, though there is a lot of work for us to do.

MANY MEETING TECHNIQUES ARE OUT OF DATE

Even people who try hard to have a positive influence on plans and decisions that may affect them often leave meetings feeling frustrated. This may be because the meeting was badly managed or the speaker incompetent. But it may be simply that the procedures for discussion were repressive and outdated.

As an example, for more than a century parliamentary procedure, as typified by *Robert's Rules of Order* (General Henry M. Robert, 1876), has been the guiding methodology in conducting most public meetings. Robert's "rules" are a set of guidelines for organizing and conducting meetings with civility and dispatch. Basic to these rules is the "motion." At many points during a meeting participants can make "motions" to do or not to do something. A "debate" follows, wherein participants can only discuss the merits of the proposed solutions. The group usually cannot explore other possible solutions until they vote to accept or reject that motion. The motion can be amended but this only refines the original proposed solution—it cannot be radically altered. They can choose to "table" the motion, but they cannot open a search for fresh, creative alternatives. Because of these constraints, many people in positions of governance resolve their conflicts through horse-trading behind closed doors, thus excluding the membership of the meeting or the public in general from the real process of decision making. This in itself frequently leads to angry people.

The procedures offered by Robert's Rules limit a group's ability to develop and apply innovative solutions to the increasingly complex problems that develop in today's world. The *motion* may force a group into an "either-or" kind of choice that may not meet the needs of many of the participants as well as might be the case if other problem solving methods were used.

There are several other meeting practices that we commonly use without real appreciation of the difficulties they can cause us. For example:

• *Voting*. Voting also gives an either-or choice, and requires that up to half the members go home disappointed. This win–lose approach means that the membership must divide into opposing camps, and those in the minority often go to extremes to change their fellows' opinions or prevent the vote from occurring. Upon losing, they may attempt to undo the decision if that is possible. For the losers, voting often leads to resentment, a sense of defeat and a hopeless-helpless feeling.

I am not against voting, and people rightly fear the vote that is final. Voting is better than deadlock or chaos but in many cases it is unnecessary. It often assumes that we can't creatively develop a both–win solution to controversy.

• *Compromise.* We have enshrined compromise as the most artful way to solve disputes. Compromise is a good way to dispose of minor conflicts in a hurry, but often breeds as many problems as it solves. Compromise assumes that you must give up something and so must I; we simply bargain over who gets what. The bargaining process often takes much time and effort and, worse, we may fail to explore better options. Compromise is often a half-a-loaf cop-out. If we are creative instead, perhaps we can make the loaf better and bigger so we both get more of what we need.

• *Arbitration.* An arbitrator is selected to solve an issue when opposing parties fail to do so. But arbitration doesn't necessarily settle matters, since one party must end up the loser, or it produces a compromise. Though arbitration settles many disputes quickly, it is often a method of avoiding responsibility for settling the dispute by the participants themselves, and for the consequences that ensue. It also raises questions about the parties' problem solving skills.

• *Mediation.* A mediator is a third party who *helps* the opposing sides reach an agreement. The mediator, rather than the people with the problem, exercises negotiating skill. Though mediation is often productive, it leaves the parties to the dispute dependent and as undeveloped in their problem solving skills as ever.

• *Coin-flipping.* Though not often used, this can be a sure way to avoid deadlock, but it means flipping away responsibility and leaving the future to chance. It gets the job done, but often at a high price.

All of these techniques have some value, particularly in conducting run of the mill meetings. However, where issues are critical and tempers short, they may need to be replaced by more sophisticated methods.

OPTIONS FOR HOPE

Although some things are getting worse, others are getting better. While some tools are becoming less serviceable, others are appearing that offer new flexibility, strength, and precision.

If you are to appear before a troubled or volatile audience today, you might well find previous techniques inadequate. You need new and powerful public speaking tools, and you need to be able to wield them with finesse and confidence. You need to adopt a revolutionary attitude toward public discourse—an attitude that favors beneficial results for *all* those engaged in a controversy. You need to join the search for creative and mutually beneficial ways to resolve issues between us if our society is to solve its more serious problems.

Professionals in many fields are developing tools and methods to make your job easier. For example:

• Sociologists are providing new insights into the structure of human groups and into ways to better use their inherent creativity and diversity. Our view of what is possible in meetings is expanding as we learn more about how to generate "both–win" solutions to public and private conflicts.

• Psychologists are teaching us about our emotions and motivations so that we can lessen tensions in groups, design solutions more satisfying to all, and gain greater commitment to carrying out those solutions. These scientists are designing tools for researching, analyzing, and building empathy with our prospective audiences, and they are finding ways to help us identify and build on our personal strengths so we can become more effective leaders.

• Managerial experts, through their focus on solid objectives, can help us make our goals more explicit and set a sound base for solving problems in groups. Concurrently, they are providing new ways to plan, organize, and conduct meetings.

• Training professionals are providing new tools for making presentations more flexible, interesting, and focused. Exciting new media, are expanding the ways we can clarify, explore and resolve controversial issues in our meetings.

• Scientists and medical doctors researching stress offer a variety of easily learned skills to reduce anxiety, and improve performance when speaking to a difficult audience. By inoculating ourselves against stress, we can avoid becoming trapped in those arguments and hostile exchanges that damage so many speakers.

Overall, the behavioral sciences (particularly) continue to refine our ability to read an audience accurately, understand audience dynamics, and deal with special problems such as apathy, boredom, and indifference, as well as organized opposition and extremism. Keeping up to date will not be easy.

Out of fear, habit, or ignorance, most speakers fail to employ the knowledge these professionals offer. However, don't worry, this book offers a systematic and comprehensive summation of tools and techniques that all public speakers can use, to ensure better outcomes from the more difficult meetings we lead or coordinate. Select among them to suit your personality, circumstances, and talents. Practical guidelines for their use are included.

By learning these techniques and applying them carefully in group meetings, you can promote true resolution of the issues that divide us in our business, public, and institutional struggle—to improve the lives of all of us, as individuals, and as members of our communities.

CHAPTER TWO

Your audience:
your job

Janice K., a very tired mother of four, has to tell her children that she and their father have separated and that she is filing for divorce. She expects the older children to be angry and worried about how this will change their lives, and the younger ones to be scared and sad. She expects to be told they don't like it. She is angry at being left alone to do this job. She begins to speak . . . .

Across town, Jeff D., a police official, has rushed to a hastily arranged meeting of neighborhood civic leaders who are upset about the shooting of a youth in what is perceived, by some, to be a racially related incident. Sporadic violent outbreaks have occurred since the event and more are likely. Jeff needs the help of these community leaders to cool the area down. As he steps from the squad car some of the crowd is chanting and others are hurling obscenities. Jeff spots TV trucks nearby and knows that he will be covered live as he speaks. As he moves through the cordon of officers, the hostility seems overpowering. He enters the building . . . .

In the state capital Assemblyman Dan W. is sitting on the edge of his chair ready to begin the speech that may be his last, in that body. The elections are near and they are debating, at the Governor's insistence, a reduction in the state employees' pension fund and retirement system. He is scheduled to speak in defense of the pending bill. He believes that the present ill-conceived and uneconomic system needs to be changed. He also knows that the state employees' union has packed the galleries and that hundreds of union volunteers and sympathizers are outside the building whooping it up before the TV cameras. He hopes that the crowd will allow him to complete his presentation with dignity. He rises to speak . . . .

Carla J. has been selected to explain a controversial change in company policy. She is to serve as one of five panelists who will make presentations to groups of 200 employees at a time. Word of the changes has leaked out and distortions abound. She knows her subject well but personally dislikes the changes and is certain that her audience won't like them either. Also, the room is too small, the people are crowded, and the long, narrow space will make it difficult to establish contact with those in back, or for them to read the posters she has prepared. Worst of all, she will follow a generally hostile and combative speaker and will catch some of the flack he generates. Finally, the sequence of the presentations is likely to confuse people. She feels annoyed, lonely, and worried. The lead speaker is beginning his presentation . . . .

As our earth spins, each new day brings millions of individuals before audiences that are not all smiles and warm enthusiasm. What can these speakers, entertainers, teachers, elected officials, technical experts, government employees, parents, administrators, clerics, club officers, and many other people, who have had events and circumstances conspire to place them before a group where feelings are strong and negative, do to better manage themselves, the situation, and the people they face, so that the encounter ends as well as possible?

You are either paid to produce beneficial results from the meetings you hold, or you want your audience to meet your needs in some way that you consider important to your own ends. The problem you and I face when an audience is being difficult is often a complex one and feels unique to each of us. Sometimes we can prepare and sometimes we can't, as when an accident or tragedy strikes and one is virtually catapulted before a group of TV cameras to act as spokesperson, or reporter. No two situations are ever the same, and though we need flexibility and creativity, there are also many other ways we can train ourselves to master these situations.

YOU AND YOUR AUDIENCE

When you face an audience, by that very act you set yourself apart from them. You cannot be one of the group; instead, you are trying to accomplish something with them or through them. If your relationship with your audience is a benign one—if you are a leader, a teacher, or perhaps a supervisor—they may expect a beneficial interchange. Yet though they may see you as a friend, helper, or patron, they still see you as set apart from them in some special way.

If a majority of the audience feels strongly about the issue at hand, you become the object of their volatile emotions. You are— temporarily, at least—perceived as an adversary. How can you, set apart from your audience as you are, ensure that the encounter will end as well as possible? How can you get your job done?

You feel you are alone against the hoard. You have a duty to perform, and you'll be magnificent if you win, a fallen hero if you lose. Though you may search the room for friendly faces, pray for late arriving allies, or affect a demeanor that commands respect, you know it's you against them, and you rehearse strategies and tactics for the battle. You must win, and their losses mustn't concern you.

But must there be a winner and a loser? Are your goals really incompatible with theirs? Perhaps you should think again about what you are trying to accomplish.

DEFINING YOUR JOB

It is easy for a person standing before a hostile or recalcitrant group to be so preoccupied with self-defense that they fail to see opportunities for mutual gain.

Most people who face difficult gatherings feel they need, above all, to take control. They decide what they want, design the most obvious road to get there, and push ahead regardless of the conse- quences to those they are addressing. If the audience resists, they fight like cornered animals.

They know, of course, that high-powered oratory will not always save them, nor will brilliant repartee. Deviousness may gain the day but lead to long-term mistrust. The insult can satisfy the ego but damage the relationship. The belittling retort can whet the victim's appetite for revenge. Talking down to groups can evoke childish outbursts of temper.

These tactics waste the speaker's time and resources. Those who rely on them usually fail to meet both their real needs, and those of the people or organizations they represent. Taking control may help them reach a goal, but it should not be a goal in itself. By focusing too much on the process, they lose sight of the desired results.

Once people start thinking about what it is they really *need* from a meeting, they find themselves focusing on positive outcomes—not about the ways that they'll assure those outcomes. They begin to take a new and broader view of their job—to adopt a new vision—to consider some ways to make that vision a reality. They may stand back and reappraise the audience, the situation, and even themselves. And their desire to take control may disappear.

In redefining your role, of course, you need the support of those you represent; if you're simply told to "go out and give them hell" you can't be very creative, or accomplish anything much that is useful but perhaps you can begin to see yourself as a catalyst for achieving mutually beneficial results in the meetings you lead

When you are challenged by shrieking dissidents or harangued by petty demagogues on the floor, you need not respond in kind. When your meeting is disrupted by militant protestors or when hecklers assail you, your meeting can be recovered, your dignity restored. You can avoid being captured in an unproductive interchange with an audience member, and you can bend before a hurricane and plod steadily toward fulfilling your purpose. When your listeners are listless and inattentive, you can unleash their power and enthusiasm for useful work. Whatever troubles beset your group, you can lead them toward problem solving and conflict resolution. When they lash out at the world and its injustices, you can be a haven and a hope.

You must treat your audience with empathy and dignity. Simply showing respect for their views, beliefs, and feelings, can alter their perceptions, modify their behavior, and help them to seek new productive directions. It helps in the beginning to recognize the mutual dependency between yourself and them.

MUTUAL DEPENDENCY—
SPEAKER AND AUDIENCE

One of the best ways to see your relationship to a hostile group clearly is to recognize that you need them for your success or you wouldn't be interacting with them. If there were no challenge there would be no achievement. If you are an office seeker you want their votes. If you are presenting a controversial plan for zoning changes, you at least want to reduce the obstacles to your program. If you are announcing reductions in the company's fringe benefit plan to employees, you hope to gain their understanding and perhaps their passive acceptance of the new plan.

In the same way, your audience needs something from you, even if only to release their anger. They would probably be disappointed if you weren't there. At least some of them, however, want more. They may want you to help them gain a clearer understanding of a controversy. They may want to influence you, or, through you, the people you work for. They may hope that by making their opinions and anger known, they can improve their fate, redress a wrong, or stabilize a volatile situation.

Why should you worry about the needs of your audience? Because they have power too. If they leave the meeting feeling like losers, they may drag their feet, sabotage your plans, or get even in ways too subtle and covert to be noticed. If this happens, you will be locked into unproductive combat that will deny either of you a clear-cut victory. Unless you annihilate the opposition, you'll both end up losers. But can both you and your audience go away feeling satisfied? It is possible for both sides to emerge from the meeting feeling good about the outcome, and ready to cooperate in the future for further mutual gain— but only if the wits and imagination of the groups are harnessed for this mutual gain. Since your audience may not fully appreciate the need for cooperation, you may have to act as teacher, or guide, in explaining the potential of new ways to work together. You may need to lead the group through experiences that will demonstrate the practicality and rewards of these new ways.

Your success in dealing with a difficult audience will depend on your self-preparation, the elements of the encounter, and your particular audience. But the greatest resource you possess is your own creativity, and that of your audience. If you can set positive goals that appeal to the group, focus their energy and imagination on those goals, and facilitate their movement toward them, there is no limit to the good results you can achieve.

CAN BOTH YOU AND YOUR AUDIENCE WIN?

What is winning? Winning can be defined as a gain for us in relation to our value system. To be a winner doesn't always mean that there has to be a loser. Few issues are as clear-cut as competitive sports. If my goal is to improve my game of golf, or to lift more weight at the gym each week, I can feel like, and be, a winner each time I achieve. When speaking to a hostile group my ability to win does not depend on their losing—perhaps we can win together.

If I have important information to impart to a group I may aim to have them listen well, with few interruptions and disturbances, so they will absorb and understand it. I thus establish a value that is important to me, but I may also work myself into a trap. By focusing on the "how"—that is, that they should listen with few interruptions and disturbances—I may short-circuit my real goal, which is to ensure that they absorb and understand the information. If I focus instead on the larger goal of understanding, I may find a variety of effective ways to accomplish it. I might present the information through role play, skits, small group discussion, or written self-paced instruction. Some of these learning methods might be enhanced by interruptions for analysis, and disturbances such as enthusiastic shouts, and might result in greater learning than a lecture. If I really value learning over method, then by using the participative methods I would probably come out a winner. If they learned and enjoyed doing so, and if the experience enhanced their sense of competence, they might also leave the meeting feeling like winners.

Success means something different to every participant in a public forum—the speaker, the speaker's sponsor and each member of the audience. But at the same time success means only one thing—getting valuable results relative to the investment of time, effort, and other resources. Every one of us would like to come out of a meeting and say, "I got a lot out of that meeting" though *what* we got would vary enormously from person to person. If we each "got a lot" we'd each feel like winners, and our satisfaction wouldn't depend on anyone's failure.

Your audience will be more willing to satisfy your needs if they see there is some gain in it for them. Consequently, you must try to understand their needs, and find ways to meet them, or at least, avoid threatening them.

WHAT DO YOU HAVE TO OFFER EACH OTHER?

The art of satisfying a person's needs is not just giving them what they want (or ask for), but rather in making available to them the things that they really value.

Only the other person can tell us what he or she values and only that person can determine when he or she is satisfied. This is as true collectively in an audience as it is in individual transactions.

This means that if both you and your audience are to go home reasonably satisfied, you have to interact with them creatively until you understand their feelings, and can identify the needs from which they originate. Then you can use your talents to achieve worthwhile ends that will endure the test of time.

CHAPTER THREE

Setting objectives:
what do I want
from this meeting?

"What is your primary objective for this meeting?" I once asked a condominium manager who was about to face an audience incensed by a huge increase in maintenance and utility fees. "To get out of there alive," was his serious response.

To enhance that goal he might also consider related objectives such as "to leave under his own power and in a standing position."

If you want to set reasonable objectives for a tough meeting, begin by asking some simple questions such as: What will be my job at this meeting? Why will I be there? What will I need to accomplish? For what purpose am I addressing this group? These basic questions are important because you need to have it clearly fixed in your mind where you are going, and what you want to achieve even before you begin to consider your audience and why they may be difficult or hostile.

If you don't set your goals first, you may find yourself responding to the audience and their goals, and lose sight of your own. It is not being insensitive or arbitrary to consider your goals and objectives first, because unless you achieve what you came after, at least to some degree, you are wasting your time and effort. This doesn't mean that you are unable or unwilling to reconcile the audience's needs and your needs;

and it doesn't mean that you are, or need to be, stubborn or inflexible or ride roughshod over anyone else. Setting your goals and objectives clearly at the outset simply means that you know exactly what you are about, and that you will know when you finish to what measure you have succeeded.

WHY WILL I BE THERE?

What is my role? People address audiences for a multitude of reasons: some personal, some organizational, some for a complex mixture of reasons.* Your reasons may include any, or all, of the following and you may have others as well. Common reasons include:

- To fill time
- To explain
- To convince
- To spur action
- To present facts

- To achieve public exposure
- To get them to hold direction
- To nominate
- To narrate
- To train

There are three common ways people set objectives for their presentation, and the value of their work is affected by which type of objectives they set. Some focus on process and how it is to be presented, others on content and its impact on the audience, and a few deal with end results. A training situation provides an example of the three approaches and their consequences. One trainer says: "I want to explain the policies and procedures concerning the handling of classified materials" (a process oriented objective); the second might say: "I want the class participants to know the security procedures related to handling classified material" (a content oriented objective); while a third trainer might say: "I want to eliminate security violations resulting from mishandling of classified material" (a results oriented objective). What the trainer will do, how he or she goes about it, and the results attained,

---

*Note: Objectives for your meeting should be written down, mentally massaged and internalized to make them uniquely your own. You might begin this section by taking pen in hand and jotting down objectives, or ideas for objectives, for a meeting that you might run in the future, as a way of testing out the ideas suggested here.

are likely to be influenced by which type of objective the trainer sets. Certainly the third type of objective is harder to achieve, but if it is achieved, the value will be highest.

Another approach to setting objectives that speech writers often use is to ask themselves: "Do I want understanding? agreement? or action?" This approach is not as precise or as measurable as the first approach (in most cases) but may be adequate for your purposes. If you were trying to explain the disadvantageous changes in a company fringe benefit package, understanding may be all that you are hoping for. If you were trying to sell a group on accepting a change in work rules, agreement (at the meeting) might suffice. But if you wanted to be elected to office at a club meeting, you would not be satisfied with anything less than direct action—voting for you.

Though there are many ways to set objectives, and many different objectives that could be set for any given meeting, those that deal with clear, measurable results are generally most productive.

LET'S GET SPECIFIC

What do you want to achieve with this group, especially when it may be a difficult or hostile group? (1) You may want to be able to complete your presentation. (2) You may want to avoid interruptions. (3) You may want an indication from the audience that they not only heard, but understood your principal points. (4) You may want to provide an opportunity for participants to ask questions and clarify issues. (5) You may want general acceptance of the position you are taking on the issues by the conclusion of the meeting, and (6) you may want favorable press reports on your presentation and viewpoints. Almost all meetings require multiple objectives.

Objectives such as those above seem reasonable and worthwhile, but will they fill the bill when you face a really tough audience? You may need even more specific objectives. Let us use the following situation as an example: You are to unveil a general planning model for the year 2000 for a rapidly developing section of your community. You want to present the overall plan in such a way that the citizens understand the considerations that went into the plan, the options the planners dealt with, and some of the dilemmas faced by the community in arriving at such a comprehensive plan. Immediate acceptance of the plan is not critical at the moment because it will be up for referendum nine months from now. The plan does propose zoning changes that are likely to be considered disadvantageous by some. And, the location of a new highway interchange and a new school have already caused some public outcry based on early newspaper accounts. You anticipate that some members of the audience will come to your meeting loaded for bear.

To make some of the objectives more specific it is often helpful to ask yourself three questions:

1. What do I want to happen before the meeting?
2. What do I want to happen during the meeting?
3. What do I want to happen after the meeting?

If we use our planning model presentation we may want to add some specific objectives to the generalized list of objectives offered above, for example:

1. I want to defuse some people's concerns that this will be their only chance to speak out on their special interests.
2. I want to maximize audience understanding of the scope of the plan itself.
3. I want to turn audience objections about specific points to a careful examination of the plan in its overall form.
4. I want the audience to focus their concerns and complaints in such a way that they can, and will be, dealt with in a later meeting (thereby keeping this meeting focused on presenting an overview).
5. I want the press to help in explaining the overall plan rather than concentrating on the dynamics of the meeting itself.

Thus by making my objectives more clear-cut in my own mind, I can focus my planning to reduce the likelihood of negative audience behavior and increase the likelihood of attaining my goals. I would therefore assign objective No. 1 to what I wanted to happen before the meeting, No.'s 2, 3, and 4 to what I wanted to happen during the meeting and No. 5 to what I wanted to happen after the meeting. There are certainly other objectives you might want to achieve in a situation such as this. But these items will serve to illustrate that such specific objectives can lead to the design and preparation of a more productive meeting than is most often the case.

Though writing objectives is difficult, positive benefits can accrue from clarifying what it is that you want to achieve and in measuring how well you did. People who manage their affairs by the use of objectives often want greater precision in stating their objectives and they want them written.

Once formulated, a set of objectives for a certain type of meeting and a certain type of audience can be used over and over again, or modified to adapt them to a specific unique situation. You seldom have to start from scratch.

DEVELOPING AN ACTION PLAN FOR YOUR OBJECTIVES

There are many ways to carry out a specific objective. An objective states *what* is to be accomplished; and the consequent "action plan" for carrying out that objective deals with the *how*. It is important not to mix the *what* with the *how*, for if you do, you are likely to limit your options and focus on the illusionary "one right method" of doing something. Since we have looked at the "what we want to achieve," let's explore a *few* of the "how's" inherent in this particular situation.

First—Before the meeting, "I want to defuse the audience's concern that this will be their only opportunity to speak out on their interests." To meet this objective we might prepare a press release, or meeting notices to make that point clear, up front, for example:

> This meeting will be used to present an *overview* of the year 2000 planning model. Specific citizen concerns will be addressed in subsequent meetings. At the conclusion of this meeting citizens will be asked to identify their particular areas of interests so that future meetings can be arranged with Planning Commission personnel on each specific topic.

Because audiences often become upset when they believe their issues are not being dealt with, this sort of notice should go a long way toward helping them focus on the real purpose of the meeting. By contrast, how often have we seen notices such as:

The Planning Board will reveal its year 2000 plan Tuesday evening, April 4, 19-- at a meeting at Woodmont High School starting at 7:30 P.M.

And that's all!

Second—At the meeting "I want to: (1) maximize audience understanding of the scope of the plan; (2) have audience members focus their questions on the nature of the plan itself; and (3) have the audience articulate their fears and objections in such a way that future meetings can be planned to deal with these issues." Though the above statements recast the previous objectives somewhat, they can aid in planning specific parts of the evening's activities and influence the nature and form of your presentation.

At the beginning of the meeting you might pass out cards, on which attendees could list their areas of concern, to be turned in to you at the end of the meeting. By making such cards available at the meeting (with a supply of sharpened pencils) you automatically provide participants with (1) an outlet for ventilating feelings, (2) a chance to clarify their own feelings in writing, and (3) a reason for wanting to understand the plan. When this is done, participants tend to concentrate on matters of content or substance. If they do get off on a speech or denunciation, you can politely ask them to jot down their concerns "so that it won't be lost" and "so that you can explain the rest of the plan in full measure without spending the whole group's time on issues that will be addressed in more detail at another time." You could also say that "I fear being sidetracked so that the people here will not get a full understanding of *all* of the issues in this plan."

Third—"I want the press to help clarify the overall plan rather than to report on the dynamics of the meeting" (and the problems I encountered). This objective also could be met in a variety of ways which are limited only by your imagination and resources. For instance, you might provide members of the press with a simply written (journalistic style) summary of the overall plan the way you intend to present it. This could include a clear map or table that would highlight and clarify the principal parts of the model. Since the cards on which the participants listed their areas of concern would have to be tabulated and analyzed, this process could be described, rather than the concerns themselves being dealt with in detail in the media. Since reporters, like everyone else, find it helpful now and then to have part of their work done for them, there is a good chance that they'll use your material rather than creating a whole story from scratch. Also, the eventual report on the participant cards and their concerns, promises the reporters another story at a later date.

You might object to the above scenario by saying that this meeting could lead to several others. True enough, but consider that the purpose of this meeting was to achieve *understanding* of the plan and your chances of accomplishing that objective are good—whereas otherwise you might have had an inconclusive meeting with questionable results. Also, since your overall goal is to get the final planning model approved and implemented, those other meetings would probably be required anyway. Also, the chances are good that the progress of those future meetings would be clouded by misunderstandings or the less complete knowledge held by the participants. Finally, the cards could give you data on the size and type of problems you are likely to run into in the subsequent meetings—each of which would concentrate on more clearly stated and understood obstacles to your overall goal achievement.

THREE PARTS OF AN OBJECTIVE

For full development of a written objective we need three parts: "Action(s)" (what is to be done or accomplished); "Result(s)" (how we know it is accomplished); and "Constraint(s)" (or Condition(s)). For example:

> "To conduct a one-hour training session on the new fire inspection procedure so that participants can fill out form 189 correctly by the end of the session." This objective, which may have to overcome audience boredom and apathy, nevertheless has the three required parts of a complete objective. It has an action of "conducting a session," a result (stated and implied) of "filling out a form correctly," and a constraint (or condition) "by the end of the session."

A well-written objective starts with the word "to" followed by an action verb. Examples are:

to introduce   to conduct
to limit   to analyze

to convince	to decrease
to organize	to establish
to increase	to implement

These introductions are followed by *actions*, *constraints* and *results* and deal with what is to be done or accomplished, such as:

1. To introduce participants to the new time keeping requirements for supervisors.
2. To limit the program to exactly fifty minutes.
3. To convince my listeners that the new law can make their jobs easier.

To check the completeness and value of a formal, written objective we need to ask:

1. Is the action stated specifically—do you know *what* you will be doing?
2. Are the results measurable or verifiable? Will you know when you have achieved your objective?
3. Does it list the constraints or conditions such as monetary or time deadlines, or human limitation under which you will be working?
4. Is this objective consistent with the other objectives you have set for your presentation?
5. Is the objective realistic and attainable?
6. Is the objective helpful to you in carrying out your mission?

These six questions can ensure that your objectives help you to achieve your overall goals.

A BALANCED SET OF OBJECTIVES

The principal value of having a solid set of objectives for your meeting is that it helps you to plan your presentation and your activities better. They also allow you to tie your methods and media to the objectives so as to more likely get what you want out of the meeting. Good objectives keep you on track, tell you how you are doing, and help you to build an effective presentation.

Important! You need a *balanced set* of objectives which cover all the important aspects of your meeting. To search for the one great objective is a delusion—it can mean that you achieve that goal at the expense of other, equally attainable goals, and often encounter unresolved problems at a later date.

Finally, a good set of objectives tells you clearly "when this meeting is over." When you've met your objectives as well as you can hope to, it is time to go home.

CHAPTER FOUR

Structuring your meeting for positive results

The objectives you have set virtually determine the type of meeting you'll be holding. There are four basic types of meetings; these are:

- Informational
- Persuasive
- Advisory
- Problem solving

This distinction is important because it can help you to keep clear the direction in which you want to go; the things you need to do to get there; and how to take maximum advantage of the strengths of each type of meeting. It helps you to better plan your session, organize your resources, and play out your part in the meeting. The type of meeting you use not only helps you to meet your objectives more directly, but it can help you to keep a negative situation from becoming worse. A professionally run meeting is characterized by an absence of irritants, delays and flubs. A clear focus on the essentials of your meeting structure can add that professional touch to your efforts.

The type of meeting that best promotes your objectives carries a lot of built-in structure with it, as well as opening up the opportunities inherent in that type. For example, an informational meeting virtually mandates a well organized presentation whereas an advisory meeting is often very amenable to a freewheeling session which uses brainstorming techniques to gather ideas.

WHAT TYPE OF MEETING?

"Holding a meeting" often means two quite different things to people. Sometimes it means a more or less regular or normal gathering of people to conduct some type of business, such as a manager's weekly staff meeting or the monthly Parent–Teacher Association meeting. This type of get-together is often at a scheduled time and a variety of issues might be dealt with. These meetings usually fill up the time allotted no matter what is discussed. The other type is the special meeting where people come together to deal with a special issue of interest to them, or a group of closely related issues. These meetings are usually goal oriented, often possess a sense of immediacy, and are often unpredictable, as far as the time is concerned.

Many meetings, take too much time because they lack clear-cut objectives and effective procedures.

However, a meeting that covers a certain block of time may have several, quite different topics to deal with, each of which can benefit from its own objective and consequently from its own particular kind of meeting procedures. Thus, an agenda that lists three topics may mean three objectives (one for each) and consequently three distinct types of meetings, even though they are all contained in the same time frame, e.g., within the manager's weekly staff meeting. Thus, at a well run general meeting you may have in effect three mini meetings each using quite different approaches or procedures. It is this failure to select appropriate meeting formats, and procedures for each segment, that often leads meeting managers into a quagmire of inefficiency. Therefore, develop your objective(s); select the type of meeting that matches your objective(s), and then use the appropriate meeting procedures and methods to achieve your objective(s). A well-written objective will almost always clearly identify what type of a meeting (or meeting segment) you need to get that objective across.

1. In a potentially volatile situation "To explain the decline in health benefits in the new contract to the hourly employees," signals an *informational* meeting, or meeting segment.
2. "To convince the union membership to accept the company's latest wage offer" is clearly an objective for a *persuasive* meeting.
3. Similarly, "To gather suggestions on how to move the drill presses without interrupting production" indicates an *advisory* meeting.
4. In planning a business meeting where project cost overruns are likely to be a hot subject, an objective statement such as: "To decide whether or not overtime will be necessary on the KY2-123 project" casts the meeting in a *problem solving* mode since a group decision is implied.

A further advantage of this approach, of moving from the objective to the type of meeting, is that you almost automatically clearly signal the theme and even a lead-in statement for that meeting or meeting segment.

Therefore, using the examples given, a possible lead-in statement for each meeting or meeting segment that might develop the theme could be as follows:

1. *Informational.* "I want you to *understand* the changes in the health benefits that are in the new contract."
2. *Persuasive.* "I hope to convince you that accepting the company's latest wage offer is vital to your own interests."
3. *Advisory.* "I'm here *to gather your suggestions* on how to move the drill presses without interrupting production. I'll pass your ideas on to the plant manager for a decision."
4. *Problem Solving.* "We are here this afternoon to *decide* if overtime will have to be authorized on the KY2-123 project."

It is important that people have a clear idea of the type of meeting they are attending so that their role and responsibilities are as clear to them as yours will be. This type of lead-in statement begins this process of understanding.

If people do not clearly understand the type of meeting they are attending they may entertain false expectations and become very angry when they come to believe that they have been conned. For example:

I've seen several advisory meetings where the participants did not understand that their role was strictly that of giving advice or suggestions, and that the decision was to be made by a higher level authority, based on additional information from other sources. Because they thought they were in a problem solving meeting or that they were involved in the decision making, they became hostile and resentful when the decision came from above or seemed to ignore their contributions. Carrying the objective through to the thesis statement, and having the type of meeting you are conducting very clear, helps prevent that type of misunderstanding.

THE INFORMATIONAL MEETING

Here you want to impart information that may be controversial, easy to misunderstand or misinterpret, and which may be ignored or rejected. However, you want to be able to deliver it and have it at least understood and preferably accepted. You are there to help your audience *know* and *understand* facts, information and positions that they can use to make decisions in their own minds. You may also want to keep further discussions focused on reality rather than rumor or gossip and to stimulate them to action.

To do this you may need verbal or nonverbal feedback from the audience to tell you how successful you are in getting your message across. To get the feedback you may use observation of nonverbal clues, question and answer sessions, quizzes or questionnaires and requests for verbal feedback from participants.

The key to an effective informational meeting is a clear, well-organized, and well-structured speech or presentation, with all parts flowing logically. The presentation, if possible, should be supported by visual aids and other effective devices which provide structure and development and reinforce learning. You are responsible for ensuring usability of the information by your audience.

The timing and pace of your presentation is also important. You should consider use of a detailed plan and you should practice to smooth out the rough spots. Every effort should be made to make your message as lively, interesting, and memorable as possible. This is where the level of your professionalism will be revealed.

THE PERSUASIVE MEETING

The persuasive meeting is used when you have something to sell or when you want your audience to accept your ideas or point of view, and perhaps to act on them. Your goal here is to convince your audience to give up, or modify, their individual beliefs on this particular subject, and to agree with you, at least to some extent. Hopefully you will influence them to agree with your position. You at least want to prove your point and have your position accepted as valid. At a bare minimum you are trying to make your position believable and understandable.

Some people get shy about admitting that they are involved in persuasion, for fear it smacks of manipulation. However, when you go before a hostile or difficult audience of course you want something to change—you want to influence them or the situation, and because they are involved, you have to influence them to get the change you need. This influence need not be negative, but it doesn't help to deny that you are trying to effect some sort of change in the group. The persuasive meeting (as we will see) is not the only way to bring about beneficial change in a turned off group, but when you want to effect individual or group change no other type of meeting is so direct.

In persuasive meetings the pattern of delivery and response is quite different from other types of meetings. The content is often less substantial and more emotional. Though logic is used, the story is more often told with anecdotes and metaphors. The message tends to be more vivid and powerful, and so is the response. The goal is frequently to create a type of stimulus and response communication as the meeting takes shape.

However, the most important thing about a persuasive meeting derives from the type of logic used to prove your point. A persuasive presentation must move reasonably well from beginning to end and therefore the order must be that which makes the idea acceptable. For structure, deductive or inductive logic can be used.

Deductive logic is the most commonly used. It is where we infer from a general rule or principle to reach a conclusion; that is, consequences are derived from general principles (that is, "if all men are created equal, slavery is wrong"). In public speaking we try to get agreement on the premise (or we assume it) and then we direct the facts to support our inescapable original conclusion. For example, we might start with, "The party in power is ruining the country," and then we would select the best supportive facts we have and build these to illustrate our point, so clearly that our listeners could come to no other conclusion. Our basic premise would be stated or implied in our speech at the very beginning. Then we would marshall our arguments to hammer it home. Usually our concluding statement would either summarize our main points or we would simply restate the basic premise—thereby producing a well–rounded dissertation—which has a sense of completeness.

Inductive logic is less common and deals with reasoning from the particular to the general. Here we build a case by reasoning from individual facts to universal truths or principles, that is, we lead an audience step by step from examining detailed facts to an inescapable general conclusion. For example, a candidate for political office might begin by reciting a series of easily recognizable economic ills; the inflation rate, high interest rates, unemployment statistics, productivity losses, factory closings, etc., and conclude that "it is time for a change." The primary difference between the two systems of logic is that here the premise would not be stated first, but would be developed from the facts. Though this is the type of logic we often use as individuals to come to our *own* general conclusions about things in life, there is always the risk (from the speaker's viewpoint) that their audience might reach a contrary conclusion. That is, they might add up the facts differently.

Franklin D. Roosevelt's slogan "Don't change horses in the middle of the stream" was a successful effort to undercut his opponent's inductive argument that the country and the world were going to hell in a handbasket. Both were using the same set of facts, but Roosevelt stated his premise first and supported it, while Willkie listed the world's woes and came to the conclusion that things were too serious to not make a change. Inductive logic seems to be a favorite approach of experienced debaters and clergymen. Here the speaker starts with an open-ended approach and the theme or thesis of the argument is stated last.

The significance of these two different approaches is that the inductive approach offers the best hope for dealing with a hostile audience. Just as automobile salespeople often start their sales pitch by getting the prospect to make small inconsequential decisions, the customer is led step by step to an inescapable logical grand choice. However, the inductive approach is also the hardest to construct and to control.

When a public office seeker is ranting before a friendly group they agree in advance on the general premise and all they want to demonstrate is that this large crowd agrees—in the hope that this unanimity will persuade the casual observer. Since a lot of people are undecided or ambivalent, and may already at least partly agree with the speaker's basic premise, deductive logic can be used effectively.

But where an audience does not accept your basic premise or is hostile to it, you may need to get them to reexamine the facts in a new light and reach a new conclusion. By not stating your thesis or premise in the beginning you do not risk turning them off or making the situation worse. You begin by getting them to examine specific (usually carefully selected) facts with which they agree and then lead them (you hope), to a friendly conclusion.

This type of audience interaction is not necessarily manipulative, dishonest or negative. It may be asking people to open their minds to new conclusions about facts upon which you and they agree. Few conversions would occur without this approach.

THE ADVISORY MEETING

An advisory meeting is generally called when "management" or the "authorities" need to get ideas, information, or suggestions for their own decision making process. A difficult audience at such a meeting may be concerned about the perceived effects of the subject being discussed, or they may be angry because of a past disregard for their viewpoints or concerns. In either case this type of meeting is fraught with hazards and opportunities.

The primary purpose of an advisory meeting is to obtain advice, ideas, or information that someone else (usually higher authority) needs to make a decision, solve a problem, or initiate a course of action. It is sometimes used to garner facts and opinions, to gain the knowledge or expertise of specialists, or to test a possible course of action for public acceptance.

An advisory meeting is most helpful when the knowledge needed to solve a problem is scattered throughout a group and that knowledge is hard to pinpoint—as is often the case with a general problem. An advisory meeting can be helpful when the ideas generated have to be compared with other precise data that is not generally available to the group, before a decision can be made—that is, when the decision maker has to take into account viewpoints and facts from the sources other than the group. This type of meeting is also used when the "leader" wants the group to feel involved in the decision making so as to gain greater acceptance of the decision when it is made. When you are trying to develop a program that hinges on public acceptance, having the audience who will be affected by it contribute to its development can go far to prepare public acceptance, if it is clear that their ideas did indeed influence the final results.

The greatest hazard in advisory meetings is that the leader, or the authority figure(s) he or she represents, have their minds already made up on the subject—or that the situation is perceived (now or later) by the group members in this way. Where the meeting is aimed at floating trial balloons they had better be "trial" balloons or the hostility may increase. When the meeting is held to establish the basis for greater acceptance of the final decision, that decision had better be open-ended, or at least open enough to accommodate some changes based on the group's ideas.

Speakers, or their bosses, sometimes encourage such misunderstandings, but that is a foolish thing to do. They hope that letting the group "talk it out" or "feel involved" will solve a problem. But almost always their duplicity is later discovered and thereafter the participants are not only angry, but unwilling to make contributions in the future.

The methods used in conducting an advisory meeting are critical:

- The spokesperson generally states the problem or gives background information relating to the problem.
- He or she asks the group for advice, information (on causes or consequences), ideas, opinions, suggestions, etc., for solving the problem.
- The "leader" may suggest group methods for generating and recording their inputs.
- The leader, or an assistant, generally records their inputs.
- The leader, or other person, presents a summary of what has been contributed.

- The spokesperson tells the group how their advice will be used, such as: integrated with inputs from other groups; or checked against the availability of budgeted funds; or compared with the organization's long-range plan, that is, whatever is appropriate.
- Finally, there may be (and often should be) a plan for feeding back information to the group, on what parts of their ideas can be used and what parts can not be used, and why.

The leader normally manages the discussion to get the information he or she needs. The speaker or leader may ask questions to clarify details; take action to move the group forward in their thinking; or ask the group to consider additional parts of the problem as these are exposed. The leader may also suggest group processes for generating information or ideas such as group brainstorming. The leader may also record ideas on a flipchart or a tape recorder (though some folks are reluctant to talk when a conversation is taped and can become *very* hostile if they find that the meeting has been taped surreptitiously). There may be a free exchange of information, opinions, and discussion among group members, but mostly the exchange is between the leader and individual group members.

An advisory meeting is a useful tool when a *group effort* will best produce the desired long-term results, as when public acceptance or community support is an important factor.

THE PROBLEM SOLVING MEETING

In far more cases than is commonly assumed the audience is better equipped to solve a problem than the presumed leader or expert who has convened the meeting. They may know more about root causes, more about the scope and dimensions of the problem, and far more about what they will accept as an answer to the problem. Collectively they also, probably, have more ideas about the problem than the experts do and don't know all of the reasons why fresh ideas won't work. This is particularly true when the cooperation of the audience is required to make the solution work in the real world.

A lot of problems involving other people are presumed solved by a leader working in isolation and then announced, as though that is all it took to make things happen. Curiously, many of those private decisions don't work out well in reality. Hostility flares when people believe that they have something to contribute and their potential contribution is ignored.

The primary purpose of a problem solving meeting is to develop a *workable* solution to a shared problem by using group thinking to reach a decision. This approach aims at bringing the concern, creativity and expertise of the group members together so that the solution reached is indeed *their* solution. People tend to be more committed to carrying out their own solutions rather than those of someone else. If something goes wrong they are also more likely to take corrective action if the solution is theirs.

Problem solving meetings are characterized by total group participation. Such interaction tends to be spontaneous: the group develops a solution or solutions out of a free interchange of information and ideas. The leader facilitates the group efforts and may encourage the participation of some members or suggest group procedures for tackling the problem.

Problem solving meetings as a way of reducing hostility, generating better and more acceptable solutions, and developing involvement and commitment, should be considered more frequently. Though many people avoid such meetings because they are harder to control, why, on the other hand, should a person develop a solution that encounters undue resistance, possible sabotage and even defeat?

When hostility is running so high that little is being accomplished, the leader may have few options other than to throw the meeting open to the group, or to have them identify their specific concerns and get them working on solutions. A high level of art is required to conduct a problem solving meeting when feelings are negative, but participant concerns often can be concentrated on constructive approaches and attitudes. As the group focuses its attention on the problem, anger and other emotions tend to go down. A problem solving meeting may not produce *your solution*, but they often produce high-quality answers that may very well accommodate your needs.

Generally the leader states the problem and then moderates the proceedings. The group may modify, clarify, focus, or enlarge the problem. *The leader's goal may then be to ensure that his or her primary needs are not lost in the definition of the problem or in the solutions generated.* Here the focus is on needs, rather than on solutions. Needs tend to be open-ended; solutions are closed-ended. More will be said later about this matter of needs and about conflict resolution techniques.

The leader for the most part coordinates the group's effort in:

- Defining the problem in terms of needs (rather than solutions).
- Identifying the causes of the problem(s) and assessing their nature and scope.
- Generating (creatively) possible solutions and answers.
- Evaluating the various solutions in terms of the needs of the group and of the leader. This may involve developing some further "how-to do it" ways to meet those needs.
- Selecting solutions that best meet the group's and the leader's needs. This may also involve developing some additional ways to meet participant needs.
- Planning future action and follow-up.

If handled properly, the problem solving meeting may be a creative, satisfying experience for all those involved. Such results are not guaranteed, but often excellent solutions are generated and successfully applied.

Selecting the right type of meeting (or meeting segments) for advancing your objectives and accepting the structural advantages and disadvantages that go along with it, is a large part of planning a productive meeting. Speakers who have only one option—such as to get up and harangue the audience—may be effective in achieving their *immediate* objectives for dealing with hostility and other audience problems. Nevertheless, they often fail in complex situations, and even more frequently, do not gain all of the advantages that are available to them.

A meeting that is well planned and structured to achieve solid goals lends an air of professionalism; can better support a solid presentation, and allows you to maximize your opportunities. Rather than lock you into a particular routine, a well-structured program allows you to keep your objectives on track and to make a conscious decision as to when to deviate from your plan. If you don't know where you are going, and don't keep your road map handy, you may not know when you are lost. Being aware of what type of meeting, or meeting segment, you are running at a particular moment helps you to keep your presentation techniques harmonized.

The next chapter builds on these solid meeting structures and offers ideas on how to plan a presentation for maximum effect and impact.

CHAPTER FIVE

Your presentation— achieving maximum impact

In this chapter I will tell you how to plan, organize, and write a good speech or presentation that will help get your point across with power and impact. Not bad, huh? You may already know how to do this, and if so, you can skip this chapter. *But*, before you do, consider this: Do you speak off the cuff, making it up as you go along? If so, you are probably good at it, or you would have given up that approach long ago. However, you might be even better with some planning or forethought. Such planning probably won't change your style, but it might allow you to make your points more effective and more lasting. How many times have you come away from hearing a powerful speech and said, "He (or she) was great," but later could remember little of substance?

When dealing with a hostile or troublesome audience, we need to ensure that we gain more from the exchange than "wowing" them— we want to accomplish the set of specific objectives we have set for this encounter. That takes planning, organization, and skillful execution.

If, on the other hand, you already approach a presentation in a systematic orderly way, perhaps some of the points made here can give you additional insights, or help you to refine your techniques.

Though a meeting may have several goals or objectives, and may be divided into several parts to accomplish each of those objectives, here we are going to concentrate on the preparation of a single speech or presentation.

Every public presentation, to be coherent and complete, needs a single thesis statement to keep us on track. We are often given a *subject* or *theme* to talk on at a meeting, but a thesis statement is a more precise definition of that subject or theme. The thesis statement is a sentence which sums up the central or controlling purpose or idea of your presentation. It answers the basic question, "What is the main idea I am trying to communicate to my listeners?" This thesis statement contains both the specific aim(s) of the speech, and the limitations of the subject you are going to present.

A single speech can have *only* one thesis. If you have more than one thesis, you have more than one speech. A thesis can have subtheses, but each subitem must tie directly back to the main thesis. If you can't define your purpose clearly in a thesis statement you will be likely to ramble, and include information or ideas that are not pertinent and which distract your listeners from the main point you are trying to make.

You should be able to express your main thesis in a single sentence—further clarification may be necessary, but you are in trouble if you can't express your thesis in a single sentence.

It is often a good idea to write or type this statement on a card and keep it nearby to serve as a periodic check as you develop your presentation. This will help ensure that you do not wander from your intended purpose. You may decide to change your thesis, but even then your new thesis should be written as a single sentence outlining your intent. Remember that it should contain both the limitations of the subject and the specific aims of your presentation. For example: "I plan to tell my listeners that hard financial decisions lie ahead for our county, and that increasing the sales tax and reducing or eliminating six major planned construction projects will be the best answer to our problem this fiscal year."

Your thesis statement may or may not appear as such in your speech. Your intent or purposes should be made clear, at, or near, the beginning of your presentation (unless you are using inductive logic to make your point) but the thesis statement is a guide for keeping you on track, and should not impede you from developing a dynamic or effective beginning to your presentation.

Many people have learned or inferred from somewhere, that your thesis statement is the first statement you make when writing a paper or a speech. This may or may not be true. The notion that your thesis must come first produces a hazard that many people encounter when they have both an idea of where they want their talk to go, and a real powerful beginning in their mind at the same time. Sometimes they so love their beginning that as they continue to develop their presentation, they try to shape their theme to fit their beginning—rather than vice versa. This often leads to disaster.

I often phrase my thesis statement in a way that is so awkward that I will never (or hardly ever) be tempted to use it as a beginning. That is—I begin with—"I plan to tell my listeners about. . . ."

Now if you will look back to the first sentence in this chapter you will see an example of how I violate this general approach and yet use the thesis statement to serve my purposes. I modified the "lead-in" somewhat to make it more personal, but it remains a clear statement of what I planned to do in this chapter.

DEVELOPING YOUR SPEECH OR PRESENTATION

Once you have your thesis statement in front of you, clearly written, you are ready to lay out your content in four developmental steps.

Step 1: The Body. On 3″ × 5″ cards, or on pieces of paper, list all of the examples, statistics, logic, proofs, stories or ideas that you can think of, that will tell your story or prove your thesis. It is best to do this on 3″ × 5″—one item per card—so that the cards can be easily sorted later.

Some of these may be subpoints that directly support your main thesis, while others might be ways of explaining or further developing a subpoint. It is often best to list these items as they occur to you without any initial attempt to organize them, for most people find that trying to organize ideas while thinking them up causes mental confusion and slows down or blocks the creative process.

The outcome of this step should be a sequenced array of the principal points that you want to make that support your thesis statement called major supports. Under each point you have the proofs to support that point. These can be statistics, illustrations, anecdotes, stories, jokes, and so on, that will drive home the points you are trying to make. For example, with the budget thesis statement given previously we might have the following major supports (with subpoints).

1. Our expenditures over income will produce a three million dollar shortfall this quarter.
2. Borrowing more money is impractical.
    a. We've borrowed money for the last seven quarters.
    b. Our credit is lousy.
    c. Two efforts to launch a bond issue have failed.
    d. Two major banks have turned us down.
    e. Interest rates are very high with no sign of coming down.
    f. We are, in effect, bankrupt.
3. State laws offer us only two opportunities to raise money in the amounts needed:
    —real estate taxes
    —sales or excise taxes.
4. We have raised real estate taxes for the last four years in a row.
5. A voter referendum to prohibit an increase in real estate taxes failed by only one percent last year.
6. Another real estate tax increase will surely make the referendum a success this fall.
7. A one percent increase in the sales tax is the only way we can come close to balancing our budget this year.
8. However, even with the sales tax increase we need to reduce current outlays by 1.25 million dollars to meet our current obligation.
9. This type of quick saving can only be achieved by canceling two specific building projects and stretching out four more.
10. If we carry out these steps our budget will be in balance and we can start to recover our financial credibility.

If the speaker in this scenario sets out to convince the audience of the viability of such a plan, he or she will need to back up each and every one of those statements in the most effective way possible. For instance, in developing point two, the speaker may want to prepare a series of overhead slides showing:

1. how much money has been borrowed in each quarter and the total thereof;
2. the communities' current credit rating;
3. a review of the failed efforts to raise money through bonds;
4. the names of the banks where loans have been sought 'and the dates of the refusals, etc.

Similarly, for point nine the projects could be identified and the savings for each, and the totals, could be displayed. Jokes may be inappropriate in this situation, but analogies and anecdotes might work. There are also opportunities for graphs and charts, statistics, and examples that will help prove your point.

Later the information on these cards can be converted into an outline of your speech if you plan to use one. This would produce a master plan for your presentation.

Step 2: The Conclusion. On another card (or sheet of paper) write out what you want your audience to: *understand*; *agree to*; *remember*; or *do*. This is your *plea* card. It should state clearly and distinctly what you are aiming at. It also embraces the ending of your presentation— the "tell them what you've told them" part of your talk.

You ought to consider at least seven things when you approach the end of a speech or presentation.

1 Give your presentation a definite ending. Bring your speech to a logical conclusion and/or tie it all together. Avoid uncertain closings such as, "There is a lot more I could say about this if I had more time."

2 If your presentation is long, complex, or contains many points, you may want to summarize your principle ideas. This reminds your listeners of your major points and enhances the possibility of their retaining them.

3 Don't end your speech with an apology unless there is absolutely no way to avoid it. If an apology is necessary for any reason, try to get it over with early.

4 You may want to conclude with a restatement of your thesis statement, for example: "As I said before, there are no easy choices— spending, particularly on construction, must be cut and income from a larger sales tax must be accepted.

5 Drawing a logical conclusion, inductively or deductively, from the facts you have presented, is especially effective if you have set out to defend a point of view or to win an argument.

6 Don't end your presentation by *branching* off into another aspect of the topic, by introducing new material, or by rambling to a standstill. These things destroy the sense of completion so vital to an effective presentation. The end of your speech should conclude what you have already said—and no more.

7 It is a good idea to write out your final sentence and memorize it. Make this last sentence memorable and even quotable. Ultimately it should reinforce your theme or thesis so that your audience has your viewpoint or ideas in a nutshell. End on a strong note.

Finally, if you want your audience to do something (vote A on Referendum No. 4) tell them that, and even tell them how to do it, if that is necessary.

Step 3: The Introduction. Now that you have developed your thesis in a clear orderly fashion, and have decided how to end your presentation effectively, go back to prepare a powerful beginning.

Why write the beginning after you have written nearly all the speech? Three reasons stand out: Writing the beginning last keeps you from "locking in" on a clever beginning that may make it difficult to develop your thesis logically. You have already massaged your information and your ideas thoroughly and are very familiar with them so that you can now design a better, more appropriate, beginning than is likely to be the case otherwise. More creative and original ideas are likely to pop into your head at this point since your mind has more ideas to work with.

Many people have a hard time getting started because they are waiting for that flash of brilliance that will produce an earth-shattering classic opening. That flash may never come, and while you are waiting you can get a lot of productive work done by starting elsewhere. Important as your opening statement(s) will be in the final draft, don't worry about that at first.

The beginning of your presentation should grab your listeners' attention and catapult them into the heart of your subject. This "kick–off" should be: as hard–hitting, and as attention–getting as possible; clearly launch your subject on its merry way; and be as short as possible.

Additional guides that are often helpful are: Make your beginning self-explanatory and independent of your topic's title; avoid a rambling beginning that delays getting to your principal point(s); avoid all beginnings that have nothing to do with your thesis statements, especially complaints, apologies and jokes that don't relate.

If you have trouble getting a good beginning, try one of these (and work to improve it as your day of reckoning approaches):

1. A direct proposition or statement of opinion.
2. A relevant quotation.
3. A (short) story, incident, or anecdote.
4. A striking fact or detail that will startle and get your listeners thinking along the lines that you want them to follow, or
5. Your thesis statement. Here we are primarily trying to arouse their interest in you and your presentation. For example: "Grass may yet grow in the main streets of our cities; our factories may lie idle, and our people may suffer great want if we do not face our budget crisis squarely and effectively."

Step 4: Pitching to Your Audience. Sometimes it is necessary to make an extra effort to involve this particular audience with your subject, and with your viewpoint, particularly if they are apathetic or sullen. Therefore, directly after your hot-shot beginning, you may want to show each member of your audience just why this subject is important to them. You are attempting to lure, entice, or demand your listeners' personal involvement in your presentation. You might offer the benefits to be derived from your approach to the problem, or level with a skeptical group at the start, or tell the consequences of their current course of action. For example: "My proposal does not offer any easy way out, but it does provide for a solution to our debt problem and the road to fiscal responsibility." A special effort to bring your audience in is worth the time you spend to develop involvement.

GAINING ACCEPTANCE
OF YOUR IDEAS

Your purpose in addressing a hostile or difficult audience is to influence them in some way and perhaps to change them if that is possible. You may wish to alter their attitude, their understanding, their behavior, their knowledge, or their belief. To do this powerfully and effectively you have to develop your material, your ideas, and your point of view, in a way that your audience can readily comprehend, internalize, and use. Listed here are ten suggestions for achieving impact and effectiveness.

1. *Use the Power and Rhythm of Good Structure.* A well-structured and developed presentation will flow so effortlessly that the structure will not be noticed by the conscious mind. But a person's subconscious mind will find the flow and grace appealing and relaxing. Therefore, you can develop almost a cadence or rhythm that will help to soothe the savage beast. Speak naturally; vary your tone, volume, and speed for emphasis and rehearse aloud to discover ways to smooth your flow of words.

2. *Use Consistent and Logical Reasoning.* A presentation must move sensibly from beginning to end, whether you use inductive or deductive reasoning. Your type of logic provides a structure and an order which your listeners can follow. It keeps you on track and builds to a crescendo.

3. *Use Well-Chosen Examples.* Good examples of what you are getting at make your presentation come alive. Well-chosen examples spice up your talk, make your points recognizable and connect your ideas and points with things that are familiar to your audience. These "for instances" make *you* familiar, reasonable, and perhaps believable.

4. *Stories.* A well-chosen story that clearly ties in with your presentation, or illustrates one of your principal points, provides a memorable experience. Don't make them: too complicated, too subtle, too long, or too frequent. Get to the point quickly and move on (but don't rush). Pause when they begin to react. You may want to keep a 3" × 5" card file on good stories you have heard or read about or even ones that have occurred to you. However make sure they relate to the principal point you are making and use them to advance your thesis. A difficult or hostile audience won't put up with a great deal, but a good story now and then can give you punch.

5. *Jokes.* A witty joke *can* relieve tension, loosen up the group, and even change the mood. However, a badly choosen or badly told one can grate on their nerves, produce resentment, and evoke negative behavior (cat-calls, etc.). Knowing your audience, being sensitive to their agenda and concerns, and selecting a joke that creates a common bond between you and your listeners, can go a long way toward winning the day. You may also want to consider the 3" × 5" card file for fresh, pointed jokes that express your viewpoint.

6. *Numbers, Statistics, and Percentages.* Numbers in various forms can be a powerful way to prove your point(s), demolish contending claims, and establish your credibility. However, a lot of people have learned that "while figures don't lie—liars figure." The source of your statistics is an important part of their viability. Use "good" numbers or they may come back to haunt you—particularly if you are likely to be quoted in the press or on the air. However, don't use too many numbers, especially avoid long lists. Round off numbers to easy–to–understand approximations, but acknowledge that you are talking about "approximately 80% of the adult population," etc. Support your figures, use reliable and respected sources and quote your sources. Look for unusual numbers or figures that can be integrated conceptually with your material to produce an exciting or memorable idea.

Remember, numbers are symbols that must be comprehended and translated by your listeners into something meaningful to them. Your job is not only to provide the numbers but to aid your listeners in making this translation. Focus attention on the *point* your numbers make. Relate your numbers to things that are meaningful to your listeners, especially things in their everyday lives (i.e., inflation in the last year has eaten away one-tenth of the food you put in your shopping cart).

7. *Comparison and Contrast.* One way to use numbers and number concepts, as well as other ideas that have dimension, is to put them

alongside something else and let folks "see" how they compare. The trick here is to get something that your listeners can easily relate to. A classic example is to compare wage rates between the USSR and the United States by measuring how long it takes the average Soviet worker to earn a pair of shoes or other consumer goods.

8. *Quotations, Testimony, and the Use of Authority.* Audiences are often mentally challenging the speaker with a lot of "says who?" If you use quotations well, you can answer that question effectively. While a hostile audience may well doubt your honesty or objectivity, they are less likely to do so when you are quoting a widely recognized authority.

If you are using testimony, make sure that your *authority* is considered an expert in that field and one who is not an extremist. This type of testimony supports questions of fact where issues are provable. It may be necessary to build the credibility of your expert into your presentation before such authority is used.

Quotations from literature, historical figures, and from great men and women, have considerable impact on some people. Such quotations, particularly if your listeners can identify with the source of your quotation, can have considerable emotional effect.

9. *Similies and Analogies.* These direct comparisons of (two or more), things that share one common aspect, but are unlike in other ways, can be used to give variety and visualization to your words. "Talking to those critics is like serving lunch to 'Jaws' and family."

10. *Audio and Visual Materials.* Careful consideration should be given to using viewgraphs, flipcharts, 35mm slides, and other visual techniques for illustrating any of the nine preceding methods of developing your material or proving your point. With imagination and experience well-designed visual aids can move your presentation along, keep you on track, and make your points more memorable. They offer a note of competence and professionalism.

In a similar manner, audio tapes, closed circuit TV, and movies can be used effectively to support your contentions. Not very much of that sort of thing is currently done because of the cost (real or imagined), the need for equipment, and uncertainty about the facilities you'll be using.

The first nine items listed form a checklist of supports for your principal points. Each point should be examined again to see how those supports can be made graphically, auditorily or visually powerful.

In conclusion, a systematic approach to developing the principal points in your presentation, and then enhancing each one with appropriate techniques, can produce a powerful and productive presentation.

CHAPTER SIX

Media
and Method

Most speakers treat a problem audience the way they treat any audience, only more so. They tend to do whatever they do best. If haranguing is their best suite, they harangue louder. If they lecture well, they lecture longer. As far as it goes, this approach may be useful, but they often fail to consider other approaches.

A politician who is good on the stump finds that this approach usually works well and consequently does the comfortable thing. If things don't go well, such a person often comes away from the platform feeling dejected and may wallow in self-criticism. Such negative feelings and self-flagellation often lead to determination to do better the next time, meaning more of the same, rather than the exploration of alternative routes to reach such an audience.

I once saw a magic trick demonstrated in a novelty shop which, I realized, illustrated a principle that was the central theme of a presentation I was to make a few days later. The group I was to address had been beaten to a psychological pulp by their previous management and then their company had been sold to a conglomerate that most of them had never heard of. They were justifiably afraid for their jobs and were so uptight that it was painful. The new Executive Director had spoken to the group and assured them of a bright future, but he did not believe that his words had been really effective. Now I was to inspire them and lead them down the path to righteousness.

When I entered the room most were holding themselves so tightly they could hardly breathe, or they were squirming as though they wanted to make a mass break for the restrooms. But I was ready for them. I had purchased the paraphernalia for the magic trick and had practiced it until I could carry it off flawlessly.

After a few introductory remarks and a couple of jokes that sank like Aunt Tillie's biscuits, I began to perform the trick. Most regarded me as fit for the loony bin. But the trick produced a surprise and then a roar of laughter. I then related my theme for my talk to the trick and showed them how the trick was carried off. I pointed out that all such magic was reproducible if they knew how, and that the trick of getting along in their new situation was to understand the inner workings of a system that, at first, seemed strange and even magical. I then got them involved in an exercise where they had to talk to each other and address the problem of how they were going to successfully handle their new situation. Within thirty minutes the tension was gone and they were beginning to interchange with their new management. Today, ten years later, most of them are still with the firm, and the organization is prospering. If, when inviting them to shed their protective armor, I had given one of my usual inspirational kick-off speeches, it probably would have gone over as limp as a wet sponge.

How do we systematically explore alternative routes to making effective speeches and presentations that open up new possibilities? Basically we can go back to our meeting objectives and organize our search around those. We need to investigate ways to enhance our point(s). In this discussion I'll focus on the conventional media, such as motion pictures, slides, flipcharts, and the like, because presenters often are most familiar and comfortable with these. However, your everyday world abounds with objects and gimmicks that can be used to drive home your point(s).

MEDIA CAN BE ANYTHING

I once worked for a man who was a genius at inventing ways to make his main points memorable. In teaching a work simplification and methods improvement course, he used everything from an actual street-size stop light, potatoes (one per participant), peanuts, bricks, toy parachutes, dice, miscellaneous junk from a hardware store, and a wide variety of simple games of his own invention to illustrate principles he wanted participants to remember. Some of this "media" (for that is what it was) he used was hokey, but he usually got a laugh and the people *remembered*. The fact that I can remember not only the artifacts, but the principle or lesson they stood for after more than 20 years, indicates the power of the media he selected. Whatever device, gimmick, or activity brings you closer to your objectives can be classed as media. Each of us can develop the habit of listing our principle points and then looking about us for things or methods for illustrating each point and making each memorable, vivid or interesting.

The primary reason that we should not limit our search for effective media to only audiovisual devices is that different people *learn and* consequently remember things in quite different ways. The three primary differences between people are:

1. Some people are *visually oriented.* They get much from pictures, maps, diagrams and video tapes. Much of the media that presenters use is in this category while they themselves present the audio supplement—their voice.
2. Some people are *kinesthetic.* They learn best when they have a chance to touch, grasp, hold or feel an object. Some of these people also are into emotions to a high degree, and are often sensitive to how people "feel" about each other.
3. Some people are primarily *auditory.* They deal with sounds and are sensitive to inflections in your voice, noises and conversation. They tend to listen well and are interested in the words you use, the variations in the pace of your talk, and in the concepts that are explained verbally.

These three categories are not mutually exclusive as most people learn how to learn from all three types of messages. However, studies of speech patterns and word choices indicate that most people have a preferred way to learn, a way that they are not only most comfortable with, but also learn from faster, and better than they do from other techniques. Therefore, if we want to get your message across to all members of your audience, you may want to use a variety of media to drive your points home. Media should be three-ply, visual, auditory and kinesthetic for each *major* point, whenever possible, to fully affect an audience. Compromises will have to be made at times but three-ply media can be very useful.

USING CONVENTIONAL MEDIA
AND METHODS

You, the presenter or speaker, are your prime medium. How you behave, act or speak is the most important part of the message as far as most of your audience is concerned. You are also the most versatile media. Your power to project as a living human being, to field questions and to alter the program as needed, can not be duplicated by any of the other devices you might use. You can add (or detract) immeasurably to any presentation and many of your aids and devices should be built around that fact.

However, poor use of audiovisual and other media can irritate an audience. Because there are countless ways to make a particular point, you want to use visual aids, small group discussions and other techniques that will defuse anger, enliven your presentation, reduce tension, challenge their imagination, sell your message, or even possibly dominate the group. Activities and small group work will be dealt with more fully in other chapters but they should not be overlooked when we are planning how to make our points.

Much of what is available to us is multi-dimensional. Well directed motion picture films or video tapes can appeal to both auditory and visually oriented people. This is one reason why training films often have an authority in the field, introduce the concepts verbally and then follow with a skit demonstrating the points visually. When the principle so communicated is followed by an activity involving touch or feel (such as a puzzle or a mini construction project) the learning offered becomes well rounded.

One device that you can use for looking at a variety of ways to illustrate, explain, demonstrate, support or strengthen the points you are trying to make is to construct a Methods and Media Matrix similar to the one illustrated in Figure 6–1. You can list your objectives, or things you want to do during your presentation, across the top in the sequence you plan to use them. Then for each such objective you can go down your media list and decide which one(s) would best illustrate or strengthen your point.

This matrix is suggestive rather than definitive. Your own matrix can be built around the media resources you possess or have access to. And it can be personalized if you want to focus on those methods you

METHODS AND MEDIA MATRIX

List Your Individual
Actions, Concepts,
or Objectives →

Methods
or
Media ↓

Motion Picture - Commercial																	
Motion Picture - Your Own																	
Film Clip - Commercial																	
Film Clip - Your Own																	
Video Tape - Commercial																	
Video Tape - Your Own																	
35mm Slides																	
O.H. Proj. Slides																	
Opaque Proj. Slides																	
Audio Tapes - Commercial																	
Audio Tapes - Your Own																	
Film Strips																	
Handouts																	
Flip Charts - Pre-prepared																	
Flip Charts - Outlined																	
Blank Pad and Easel																	
Blackboard - Chalkboard																	
Grease Pencil Board																	
Charts and Graphs																	
Posters																	
Samples																	
Flannel Board																	
Magnetic Board																	
Hook and Loop Board																	
Models																	
Mock-ups																	
Pencil and Paper Exercises																	
Small Group Discussions																	
Q. and A. Session																	
Puzzles																	
Physical Exercises																	

FIGURE 6–1

feel comfortable with or which suit your particular situation. For instance, if you want to introduce a new fabric to a group of employees who see this new material as a way to increase efficiency and perhaps threaten their jobs, you might want to distribute samples of material if you believe that texture, color fastness, and workability of the new fabric will help you to sell it. Additionally, you may want to update your matrix as new devices and techniques become available. This planning form, once tailored to your needs and resources, may be copied (without the top headings filled out) and used for a wide variety of presentations, even when the audience is not hostile or difficult.

In Figure 6–1, no attempt has been made to distinguish the method from the media. For example, blank pad and easel implies the use of felt pens or crayons. You can expand the list to suit your own repertoire of responses.

If you prepare such a form you can use each column of blocks as a simple checklist or you can code the items. For example, you could rank the options 1, 2, 3, or A, B, C, depending upon desirability, relative cost, ease of preparation or other factors. Or you may want to indicate more than one way to make or strengthen your point and rank them as to expected effectiveness. A dramatic example of this approach occurred at the Democratic National Convention in 1964. The Convention planners wanted to electrify the Convention and inspire the delegates to work hard during the coming election period. They prepared a film on the life and Presidency of the martyred President John F. Kennedy, called "Days of Lightning, Years of Decisions." This film had an enormous impact on the delegates. Your aspirations may be more modest, but well chosen media can make your speech or presentation a real winner.

USING MEDIA EFFECTIVELY

The selection of methods and media is firmly moving us out of the realm of the "what to do" (objectives) and into the "how to do it" phase of our planning efforts to manage a difficult or hostile audience. However, there are several other aspects of selecting and using audio-visual and other types of aids to help make your points or strengthen your presentation. These are:

1. *Offer Variety and Challenge.* The Methods/Media Matrix is a general planning document but each option is tied to a specific desired outcome. There are, however, additional benefits that derive from using a variety of media and methods that are not tied to specific objectives or activities. When we get bored our creative subconscious mind automatically produces troublesome feelings, thoughts and even actions. We shouldn't try to dazzle or spellbind people just for the fun of it, but if we don't keep their minds absorbed, a difficult audience can get out of hand. Variety and challenge in media and methods may have their own rewards.

2. *Use Experts or Authority Figures.* Just as we are our own best media, so we can benefit from the use of powerful people to enhance our presentation. More powerful than a quote from an expert is a personal appearance by that person, a recorded message, or a video tape. Special resource people come in all shapes and sizes. Use them when you can to strengthen your message or to deflect anger.

3. *Beware of Hazards Inherent in Some Media.* A short movie may be a fine device, but after lunch or dinner you may encounter the "lights out, viewer out" syndrome which is often indicated by loud snoring or people falling out of their chairs. There are ways to overcome this phenomenon, such as a stretch or coffee break before beginning, but these are not guarantees. I sometimes suggested that some participants might want to stand along the wall if they thought that would help them stay awake. Look for these kinds of hazards when you are reviewing your plan.

4. *Present or Review Your Main Points.* For example, introducing the principal points in a film may make it easier for the viewers to take in the message. Discussing it afterwards strengthens retention. Depending on your goals for the audience (learning, retention, action or acceptance, etc.), you can get durability of your message without lessening the impact.

5. *Tribulations of the Traveling Show.* If you plan to take your show on the road, make sure you allow for the problem of transporting your media or materials. While ordering your audiovisual aids from a local AV firm at your point of destination can help, a lot of tricky communication problems can arise that may cause delay in getting you

what you want. Shipping materials early or having your sponsor supply what you need often works well, but again there are risks involved. Taking items with you can mean the risk of lost or strayed luggage, a lot of backbreaking toil or porter fees. Illustrations on a large poster board can be very effective but they are the devil to carry on a windy day or to ship by air. Many people have to go on the road to explain, or implement, an unpopular policy or program across the whole organization. Take an old bit of advice seriously—"travel light."

6. *Keep Up-to-Date and Research New Options.* Wireless voice projectors are freeing speakers from the constraints of long microphone cords. Interactive video disks that offer random access to visual information offer exciting new ways to convey information. Teleconferencing, where people at scattered locations can communicate "face to face" through video screens, promises to open up a whole new travelless working world for those who frequently have to interact with groups. What the future holds is hard to predict, but people who don't keep up with the new methods and media may find themselves missing opportunities and doing things the hard way. Researching your options is no easy task, and is an endless process. However, in the critical business of dealing with a difficult audience, we need every tool and technique we can find.

7. *Avoid Very Specialized or Overcomplicated Props.* The more complicated the device, the more vulnerable you are. Do you really need that special electronic gadget? It will be harder to specify, and to get exactly what you want, from an AV supply service in a distant city. Cost generally rises and availability declines as complexity sets in. Carefully check out the implications of every device or material before you commit yourself to anything.

8. *Rehearse Your Full Presentation.* After you have decided what you are going to use, it is a good idea to go through a full dress rehearsal with all of your gimmicks and gadgets operating. Monitor everything, or have a critical and experienced observer help you by checking off every place where something could go wrong. Then go over the list and make realistic modifications to cover such adverse contingencies.

9. *Look at Yourself from the Audience's Viewpoint.* This is another place where an experienced critiquer can help you out. Can your overhead

slides be read from the back of the room? Does your voice carry in a crowd or should you augment your speaking ability electronically? Is your set-up (cords, wires, and so forth) safe and foolproof?

10. *Take Care of Details.* Provide spare bulbs for your projectors. Test plugs, adapters and equipment before use. Spot check completeness and pagination of your handouts. Avoid surprises, such as too short extension cords and the delays such things can cause. An annoyed or irate audience can be unforgiving when it comes to screw-ups, no matter how trivial. I once waited to test a film until Sunday evening. During my preview a bulb in the projector blew and I had no spare. Monday morning found me doing a soft shoe number while my ten-year-old son sped around Washington, D.C. in a taxi cab searching for a replacement bulb. Know how everything works and what you will do if something doesn't work.

One special note on audiovisual equipment: Match the equipment to the facilities. Equipment should always be set up early and its operation checked out carefully before the session. The sound and focus of a 16mm film should be adjusted beforehand, for example. The location and operation of light switches should be determined ahead of time to prevent delays and confusion. In general, if you are going to use special equipment, check out its use in the facility before you start.

The lesson in all the foregoing is "be prepared" and stay flexible.

CHAPTER SEVEN

Managing
the environment

Charlie Chaplin, in his movie "The Great Dictator," portrayed a thinly disguised Hitler. In one sequence of the movie he was preparing for his first meeting with Mussolini. An aide was showing Chaplin the arrangements that had been made to psychologically intimidate this other dictator. Mussolini was to enter a long hall, at the end of which Chaplin was to be standing behind a large desk on a raised platform towering above his rival.

The aide explained that when Mussolini arrived at the desk, he was to be offered a chair which had had the legs shortened so that Chaplin still looked down upon his rival. The aide then placed a bust of Hitler on the desk facing Mussolini so that if the Great Dictator relaxed for a moment, his rival would still have to stare at his scowling countenance. When all the preparations were in place, Hitler stood at his desk looming over the hall, awaiting his rival's entry. At that moment Mussolini swept in from behind Hitler, lustily slapped him on the back and sat down on Hitler's desk looking down at Chaplin as they talked. Not all things work out as planned.

56

POSITIONING:
THE PSYCHOLOGY OF POWER

There is power inherent in certain types of physical arrangements and in how we use such arrangements. It is equally true that advantages can be lost and hostility generated through poor physical arrangements. Being on a dais, or stage, provides a psychological vantage point in itself. Having a lectern to hold onto or to hide behind can help us to project an image of strength. By contrast, too many people in a small room where they must stand can lead to resentment and restlessness. But the use of the physical environment implies more than that.

Several years before the Polish trade union Solidarity was formed, Polish workers seized the shipyard at Szczecin during an unauthorized strike. Polish Premier Edward Gierek went to the port to try to resolve the workers' conflict with the government, only to find himself locked out of the yards. Rather than precipitate a military confrontation, Gierek agreed to enter the shipyards alone to negotiate a settlement with the workers. However, once inside the gates, he kept inviting workers he met along the way to join him at the meeting. Gierek, an old hand at group manipulation, was able to pack the meeting room with workers who had no experience with group processes, and thereby diluted the influence of the strike's organizers. By cleverly playing to the emotions of the crowd, he was able to break the firm hold of the strike leaders and win an agreement that he was later able to subvert and, through divide and conquer tactics, was able to end the unrest and purge the strike leaders.

In this instance Gierek was able to make maximum use of the environment he encountered, idle workers standing about the shipyard, and a relatively limited meeting facility, to weaken the opposition. However, his victory was only temporary and a few years later he was forced from power by striking shipyard workers determined to succeed the second time around.

The environment of a meeting can be managed to project psychological or physical power, but the efforts may be self-defeating, particularly in a democracy. Police can be used to ensure order, dissidents can be excluded, people can be intimidated, but when such

57

tactics are used we run the danger of trading off long-term results for short-term gains. When we try to use power in a free society we may get temporary concurrence, but people often reserve their right to change their mind or to sabotage the agreement through indifference or deceit. When we are dependent upon people's good will to make a plan or program work, we should be aware of the possibility of defeating ourselves by being too clever or too given to the use of power. We often have a variety of alternatives to power. However, in critical situations you may still want to structure the physical environment to gain an advantage.

FOLLOWING YOUR OBJECTIVES

The physical arrangement of the meeting environment flows as a logical step from the objectives you have set for your presentation. These objectives, and their consequent physical arrangements, should be tempered by the reality of what you plan for or expect when you are to appear before a group. If, for example, you expect that some of your adversaries might plan an organized protest to disrupt your presentation, physical security and crowd control could become an important objective in your planning.

For environmental planning, consider: (1) *The Macro Environment*; that is, the building itself, its approaches, entrances, corridors, and so on, as well as the roads or grounds surrounding it and (2) *The Micro Environment* focusing primarily on the room or rooms where your presentation will be made or your meeting held.

If you have the option, the physical environment should be chosen, arranged and utilized to maximize the *results* you are trying to achieve. Curiously, speakers or presenters are often passive about these factors and assume that the person organizing the meeting will take care of all the necessary environmental factors. Other presenters simply do not think far enough in advance to enhance their work and gain opportunities for maximizing results.

Suppose you were a political person who had overall responsibility for conducting a state level nominating convention. This convention is hotly contested, and likely to be beset by two outside special interest groups that have been pushing their program militantly at party meetings throughout the state in recent months. These two groups have disrupted several previous party meetings and have been harassing delegates in their public and private lives. Your overall objective is "to conduct the convention expeditiously; free from special interest group interference."

From this general objective could flow several specific environmental objectives dealing with such things as:

- "To restrict access to the convention center to: delegates, party functionaries, legitimate service personnel, and the media."
- "To provide security for delegates on and off the convention site."
- "To provide secure access and egress to and from the convention site for all authorized service personnel," and so forth.

It is also helpful to translate these objectives into a "needs" statement such as: seating for so many people; four nearby breakout rooms for small group discussion; prevention of electronic or other eavesdropping, and so on. "Needs" statements for the foregoing sample objectives could be, for instance: a picture pass system might be used for subobjective No. 1, along with a beefed up security force and a reduced access plan for the building. Items two and three do not imply having a guard accompany each delegate and his or her family. It may simply mean that an agreement is reached with the local hotels that guest verification and hotel room numbers, and phone numbers, of the attendees will not be given out and that attendees will have use of a sheltered vehicle space in the arrival and departure area. These needs should grow out of the objectives you have set, and can be communicated to the facility management easily once the final planning is accomplished.

In the case of a political convention, the person planning the meeting can usually get considerable help and a lot of good ideas from local police, the facilities security director, the facility manager and his or her staff, and the service organizations that usually operate within that facility. They know their locality and facility best. What they will need from you is a clear idea of your specific objectives for your meeting, and your list of needs as you perceive them. With these in hand, they are usually well equipped to design methods and systems for their facilities that will meet your needs.

How much planning you need to do depends on the seriousness of the audience problem you face, the types of outcomes you desire and the problems you want to avoid. However, there is a minimum level of environmental concerns that every professional speaker or chairperson needs to attend to, to ensure a well-run meeting. If you don't have the time, or the need, to work through a detailed set of objectives and a needs statement for your environmental planning, you can still cover the basic meeting considerations by preparing a preliminary arrangements checklist (a sample *physical* arrangements checklist is shown in Figure 7–1). Getting ahead of the game, checking out the facilities upon arrival and staying on top of changes you need to make are critical elements for a successful meeting or presentation.

Listed below are a series of steps you may want to consider for ensuring that you get the environmental support you need, yet avoid unpleasant surprises. These items represent a basic approach to facilities planning that can be expanded or simplified as needed.

Preliminary Search

Because few locations or facilities ever match your needs perfectly and some may offer opportunities that you hadn't foreseen, you may want to try to do some preliminary matching of your needs and available facilities. This might include reviewing your environmental objectives and needs statements and then checking the most desirable locations and determining what suitable facilities are available. Although your most important objectives and needs should not be shaped to fit the available facilities, some of your needs may be negotiable.

You want to eliminate clearly unsuitable situations and to identify potentially useful sites. This search may be done from file material (such as the Hotel Redbook, meeting planner guides and conference center brochures) or from your own memory. An experienced local agent or a member of your own organization who lives in the area can sometimes check out the facilities and report to you. You can call key people at your meeting site, or perhaps you only need to check out the

PRE OR POST
MEETING ACTION
MATRIX

For _____
Where _____
When _____

Date _____
Page _____
of _____

Title _____

☐ Preliminary Planning   ☐ Pre Session Actions
☐ Repeat Session   ☐ Post Session Actions

Objectives

Objective #   Objective #   Objective #   Objective #   Objective #   Objective #

Notes

Action Steps

Items Needed (Materials, etc.)

Qtys.   Dates Req.

Miscellaneous

FIGURE 7–1

61

conference room in your own facility to ensure that the room and its equipment is suitable for *your* needs.

Lists of Needs

For a complex meeting your list of needs can be long. Hopefully you have been listing your facility, equipment and special needs as you set your objectives, developed your presentation and considered your facilities requirements. All of these should be gathered into several lists to be sent to the various people who can meet those needs, such as an audiovisual supply house, the hotel meeting planner or the chief of the security agency you are to hire, etc. However, you should also investigate special needs. This may be done anywhere in the meeting planning or facilities checkout process that is appropriate. Are there provisions for the handicapped? Will smoking be a problem? Will transportation have to be provided for the attendees? If there is an overflow crowd, can the presentation be piped to other rooms? Should someone be appointed to control the lights, the projector, the electronics sound system, tape recordings, etc.? What about restrictions on having food in the room? The use of telephones and break times? Is there an emergency number where attendees can be reached? The list can go on and on, but at a professionally run meeting there is little need to explain things to your audience since distracting factors and uncertainty are reduced to an absolute minimum.

Early Communication with the Host Organization

When your audience is likely to be hostile, more is often involved in your planning than just booking a facility. Your host organization and your support service organizations need to know your objectives and needs, but they also need enough lead time to develop an effective response. You also need to define your terms and ensure that you understand what others mean by the terms they are using. What do you and your hosts mean by *nearby* "breakout" rooms; classroom-style seating arrangements, four persons to a table (does someone have to straddle the table support?), etc? Many facilities provide floor plans and sample seating arrangement layouts. Sending your host sketches of your plans improves communications.

On-Site Inspection of the Facilities

Even if you have visited the facilities during your preliminary search, you may want to return when you begin to finalize your plans. If you haven't visited the facilities yet, a premeeting on-site inspection may reveal hard seats, inadequate ventilation, poor acoustics, wretched food, inadequate telephone service, the need for extension cord adapters and a host of other realities peculiar to that facility. The importance of this step can hardly be overemphasized. Attention to detail here can prevent a lot of grief. For example, I believe that most hotel meeting planners are refugees from sardine packing plants and almost always overestimate the number of people that can be squeezed into a room. These people are trying to sell the space that they have available, their only product, and seldom reflect on the location of pillars, whether or not the sun will be in the participants' eyes during part of the day, the likely interference of kitchen noises with your speech, and other environmental hazards. You have a big stake in the outcome of your meeting and deserve to know in advance precisely what the arrangements will be and how they relate to your needs and the needs of your audience.

Walk through the facilities using the objectives and the needs statement as a checklist. Take notes on all suggestions made, or offers extended by the host organization (or others). For large and very important meetings you may also want to conduct a free-wheeling discussion and planning session with your hosts (using flipcharts to log the conclusions) to resolve outstanding issues and finalize "who does what; when and where?"

Analysis of Findings

After the facilities checkout you may want to review your findings personally or with your planning team if your undertaking is a substantial one. Give special attention to remaining problems and unresolved issues, and make as many decisions at this stage as possible. You might also develop a plan for changes (if necessary).

The need to be flexible is critical. You may need to make some environmental alterations after you inspect the site, or to obtain concurrences on your final plan from your superiors, your hosts, supporting organizations and other affected people. Finally, you may want to prepare a project planning chart and purchase orders or contracts for the facilities and support services.

Inspection on Arrival

If you are unable to inspect the facilities personally before the day of your presentation, get there early so that alterations in the furniture arrangements, and so forth, can be made, if necessary. Mistakes can be made, tasks can be left undone and intentions can be miscommunicated. Your audience, particularly if it is a hostile one, doesn't care if someone else didn't do their job. If things go wrong, they might assume that you haven't done yours. If you first arrive the night before the meeting, check out the meeting room and other facilities upon your arrival as well as in the morning before the meeting begins.

Adjustments During the Meeting

You should anticipate where the comfort level (index) of the audience will be as the meeting progresses. Should arrangements be made to increase or decrease this comfort index (if possible) depending on your objectives? Will you have someone in the room who is monitoring the environment and making necessary adjustments as the meeting progresses? If you are actually making the presentation and are also worrying about the environment, you may get distracted and/or lessen the impact of your work. Physical conditions, especially heating and cooling, can change drastically during a meeting and contingency planning for such eventualities is a must. Your responsibility to ensure that everything goes well lasts throughout your meeting.

SPECIAL CONSIDERATIONS: SAFETY AND SECURITY

Safety and security (though often closely linked) are not the same thing. Safety is a concern for the physical well-being of people and includes the health and safety of the organized opposition as well as that of your primary meeting group. The term security is often used in a broader sense which includes safety, but also includes the preservation of facilities, documents, and other property. In planning for your meeting it may be important to separate safety and security in your mind because more than one tragedy has occurred when someone forgot one or the other. For example, when someone boarded up or blocked an exit to prevent access (a security function) only to have people die when disaster struck for people could not use the exit. Separating these two functions in our mind will ensure that both are considered when planning your meeting.

Safety

Long ago most communities outlawed the act of falsely shouting "fire" in a crowded theater or other public place. However, few speakers or meeting managers really plan for the audience's safety other than to assume that local governments or building management are taking care of it.

If people plan to interfere with your meeting there is no guarantee that their tactics will consider your needs for safety, or those of others attending the meeting. Anger can lead to recklessness. Therefore it may be helpful to consider a basic list of safety items beyond those already developed when doing your facility planning.

- If trouble develops, at what point will I cancel the meeting?
- How will the building or site be evacuated, and what problems will that create?
- Who will call the police, fire department or other emergency resources, and how will they know when to do it? Who will make such decisions?
- How will police, fire, and other emergency services be summoned? Who has the numbers to call and how quickly can such forces reach the site?
- Where will (possibly) injured people be taken?
- Have alarms, sprinkler systems, fire escapes, emergency lights and fire extinguishers been located and worked into the overall safety program?
- Which, if any, aspects of the facility represent danger spots and what can be done to overcome such hazards?

This list is only a start. Many people schedule meetings or meet with hostile audiences without any significant planning. Nine times out of ten luck is with them, but people's health, safety, and life are too serious to ignore when it is likely that we will encounter serious opposition.

Security

Because disruptive groups or individuals who plan to exert pressure on, or take over a meeting, must gain access to and organize their forces for maximum impact, security and control become critical. Here the issue is, what do you want to protect or control?

A disaffected group may have planned a wide variety of actions, including: bomb threats, scare tactics, obscene phone calls, individual intimidation, infiltration, alerting the media, gate crashing, seizing control of the communications devices, and even throwing smoke bombs. We need to know a lot about them before the meeting begins. Certain overt behaviors such as catcalls, chanting or stomping, can't really be headed off if the opposition is part of your constituency or has the right of access. But at least security planning can help prevent the more serious activities.

Security planning should begin with threat assessment such as:

- What kind of organized opposition are we likely to encounter?
- What are the sources of its power?
- What is the threat potential?
- What is likely to be the size of the opposing group?
- What actions are they most likely to engage in?
- What is their history in similar situations (if any)?
- How intense are their feelings likely to be?
- What is their potential for improvising and deviating from their plan? (That is, how much uncertainty is there in the situation?)

The answers to such questions may not be ascertainable in your situation. However, if you are serious about your security planning these questions are at least starting points.

When making plans to manage your meeting environment the safety and security of everyone involved is of primary concern. You must design your own approach to managing the physical environment. If you do a good job (despite Murphy's law), your results will favorably reflect your efforts.

CHAPTER EIGHT

The ghosts
of meetings past

The anticipation of encountering a rough audience can be unnerving long before we experience the event. The fear is often worse than the meeting itself. I believe it was Mark Twain who said, "I've seen a lot of trouble in my time and most of it never happened." Feeling inadequate or unprepared can make us vulnerable, without our expected enemies making a single move.

Can I really handle this crowd? Will I be humiliated? Embarrassed? Or defeated? A myriad of such unanswerable premeeting questions may parade through our minds, colliding with our planning efforts and sowing mental confusion. The hazards can be real enough, but this self-intimidation that our mind produces is not.

These spectral apparitions arise from our past failures; legends of speaker-devouring trolls inhabiting our meeting rooms, undue attention to our personal deficiencies; and myths about perfect speakers to whom we will always compare poorly. Attention to these phantoms make us skittish, lowers our performance needlessly and causes us undue anguish. Through worry, negative speculation and self-defeating habits, we empower our adversaries, weaken ourselves and give substance to shadows.

CONJURING DEMONS

There is a certain amount of dread and apprehension that comes quite naturally when we face a threatening situation. This basic fear is used by our mind-body system to gear us up, physically and psychologically, for the "fight or flight" response. This stress response is a basic survival mechanism that we have all experienced many times.

However, there is another side to that reaction. If we learn how to handle a particular type of threatening situation, the level of stress we experience tends to go down. Thus, as we become more experienced at mastering certain tough audience situations, our level of fear and worry normally declines. This is the value of successful experience.

However, some people have acquired habits of mind and body which manage to defeat this learning process and generate self-induced stress and anxiety.

Not all of us manufacture butterflies in the stomach, nor fret ourselves unnecessarily all of the time, but most of us on occasion generate our own visions of defeat or produce anxious, unnecessary concerns.

It is not that negative possibilities should not occur to us when we are planning for a tough encounter; we should consciously list them and set forth countermeasures. However, it is one thing to face reality and quite another to evoke fearful unlikely consequences, indulge in negative fantasies, massage our vague premonitions of disaster, depress or scare ourselves by playing "ain't it awful," with others, and ravaging ourselves with unproductive circular worry.

The ways to summon negative thoughts are many, as are the emotionally based habits people use to strengthen them.

A few of these self-defeating techniques are:

Invoking Murphy's Law   We tell ourselves that "if anything can go wrong, it will," and then we proceed to imagine all of the disasters that could befall us. The "self-fulfilling prophecy" concept points out that the expectation of an event can cause it to happen (as when an anticipated shortage of gasoline or food causes hoarding and consequently produces the shortage people were worried about). This is not fate—if we expect things to go badly we will subconsciously do things to ensure that they do go wrong. We usually get what we expect.

When things do go badly, we say, "See, I told you so" and subconsciously set ourselves up for a repeat of the same phenomenon.

Strengthening the Demonic Image   We enhance our fears by playing the "ain't it awful" game by ourselves or with others. This self-generated "negative drama" sees the worst in each situation. "Those commissioners are bastards," "Those radicals will eat you up," and "You'll get some of those kooks in *every* audience," are typical expressions that exaggerate our difficulties. While making your potential opponents fire–breathing dragons is a way of hedging your bets if you fail or making a hero of you if you succeed, unfortunately, we often come to believe that baloney and do poorly because of it. A partial antidote to this self-defeating garbage is to look at the absolutes, that is, "all," "always," "never," "every," and "those" (meaning everyone) that are stated or implied in such "ain't it awful" statements, and then the falseness becomes apparent. This is how we stereotype "all" the commissioners and therefore make at least some of them worse than they probably are. If we keep feeding ourselves such extreme statements, gradually deep within us we come to believe those absolutes and operate as though they were true.

Feeding Our Worries   Worry is a negative thought process that strengthens and preserves our fears and the debilitating effects that they engender. Genuine concern, by contrast, is the legitimate caring about something that is important enough to be concerned about. Worry, however creates: (1) *circular* nonproductive thinking; (2) drains our energy needlessly, and (3) can produce a host of negative physical symptoms such as butterflies, stomach cramps, voice alterations and palpitations. We simply can't afford these byproducts of such negative feelings and thoughts.

"But what can I do about it?" you might ask. "I really have those negative feelings." True enough, but feelings are fleeting things and are inspired by thoughts. If you speculate on a negative outcome for your presentation, it is not surprising that fear and worry are close behind. But just as quickly, you can choose a positive thought which can serve to produce a more positive, productive feeling, such as: "I've handled tough audiences before and came out all right." For many people, the simple conversation with themselves of "I don't need that negative thought" (and consequently the feeling that would come along with it), and then substituting a positive thought is enough to start them on the road to strengthening their self-confidence. If additional negative thoughts keep crowding in to overpower your self-imposed positive thoughts, you may need stronger medicine. Instead of fretting yourself and working out these dread scenarios in your head you need effective ways to deal with these little devils of the mind.

YOU VERSUS YOUR DEMONS

When people try to talk us out of our worries and fears we can often cite real deficiencies to provide logical underpinnings for our self-doubts. However, we often use those realities to justify our excessive concerns, rather than as a base for strengthening ourselves.

Before you can drive out your inner demons you need to determine their names, and their dimensions or strengths. You also need to determine what you have going for and against you in this struggle.

To achieve this goal you must realistically appraise your assets and liabilities and at least neutralize your drawbacks as you build your strengths. Effective *self-appraisal* provides balance and perspective; it offers a look at both sides of reality. Such an assessment can give you the self-confidence you need but also that aura of competence that impacts so heavily on even the most antagonistic group.

To gain perspective, take two pieces of paper. On one sheet list all the things that you've got going for you—a pro list. On the other sheet list all of the personal negative things that are working against you; all of your deficiencies that could apply in this situation. *Do not* deal with your audience or their characteristics. Here, we are dealing only with you and your feelings, your inner reality.

You might want to make these lists as a general exercise right this minute. Later you might want to do it for each particular speaking engagement where you expect trouble. Don't evaluate or discount items as you write, just list all your assets and all your liabilities. Write everything that's negative and everything that's positive about yourself, that relates to giving a presentation to a hostile audience, in the next ten minutes.

When you do this listing before each presentation look for things about yourself that are uniquely applicable to each particular situation. Typically your lists may look like the following.

On the *pro* list you might have such things as:

I've succeeded with other groups;
I'm best equipped to explain our position;
I'm quite thorough in my preparation;
My voice carries adequately;
I make a good appearance;
I believe in what I'm saying;
There are some benefits to be derived from this particular plan;
The gains will exceed the losses;
People like my sense of humor.

On the negative list you might have such things as:

I get nervous;
I know they won't like some of what they're going to hear;
I stumble over some of my points;
I don't handle questions from the floor very well;
My palms perspire;
I sometimes stammer;
My stomach aches;
I get angry when they challenge me;
People walked out of my last presentation, they said it was boring;
I seem to give them more than they want.

Remember, the key to preparing successful pro and con lists is to avoid evaluating as you go along and to not discount positive or negative items, but rather just write whatever occurs to you. Get as many things down on paper as feel real to you.

In this chapter we will deal only with the negative list. In the next chapter we will show you how your list of both negative and positive assets can serve as a source of strength.

Much of our life is run by our subconscious habits; habits which require little or no conscious thought. Some of these habits are automatic functions of our autonomic nervous system such as our breathing and heartbeat. Others are learned habits such as walking, talking, and driving a car. Though we may, from time to time, give conscious instructions to our subconscious or make conscious decisions about what to do, our subconscious mind organizes the myriad of specific bodily actions that are required to carry out decisions such as tying a necktie or parking a car. This incredible subsconscious mind of ours is also where the demons dwell.

Healthy, productive habits and the feelings these engender, often live within us, alongside the negative self-defeating ones. Thus you may harbor very good feelings about your capacity to do the job you were trained for, and yet, feel very negative about having to justify a decision you made related to that job when it is assailed by a hostile group. Your confidence about your technical abilities may not carry over to personal assurance about making a speech. This collection of self-perceptions, which in most people contain some substantial strengths and grave weakness, in total, equal our self-image.

This self-image was, for the most part, formed when we were very young. Most of these beliefs came from what other people, usually our parents or other powerful authority figures, told us about ourselves and from the decisions we made about how to incorporate those messages into our sense of self. This early view of self is very strong and resistant to change, though it can grow (positively or negatively) as we encounter experiences in new areas of life where we have no prior messages. Once formed, this image guides our subconscious habits to produce the end results we envision for ourselves. Therefore, if you see yourself as a competent researcher, but a poor speaker, your mind will automatically organize your behavior to produce an excellent research study and give your stomach fits and put a quiver in your voice when you get up to present your paper. Thus, our self-image will tend to produce good or poor results for us depending on how we see ourself.

If we are going to unscramble the enigma of why our mind produces behaviors that are not helpful to us there are a few additional things we need to recognize about how our subconscious mind operates.

First, there is the "principle of consistency." In order to avoid the severe stress that would result from sudden changes in our view of ourselves (and the great changes in habits and behavior that this would require) our mind tends to select data from our environment; from our life experiences; and from within our memory banks, which supports our preexisting images. Therefore if you view yourself as being awkward before a group and you start by saying to yourself, "I'm poised and skillful," don't be surprised if a nagging voice deep within you mutters, "wanta bet?" This voice is a way of keeping you in place.

Second, our subconscious mind is very literal and it tends to accept information that is offered in the present tense as true. This is why a rote drill, such as the repetitious behavior in training people to march properly or drive cars, is accomplished by repetitive voice commands until a new habit becomes ingrained in the trainee's mind. This is also why some of the messages about ourselves that we were given over and over again as children keep coming back to us throughout our lives and why ingrained habits are so hard to break. We keep reinforcing them as we go about our daily lives. If you doubt this, listen to what your mind is saying to you during the next twenty-four hours. The chances are good that you berate yourself, despair, get angry with yourself and dwell on negative thoughts. Your subconscious thereby maintains a consistent self-image even when it is harmful to you. This "self-talk" is especially powerful if it is accompanied by vivid memories or images.

We can revise our inner thoughts about all areas of our lives and get our subconscious mind to create a new image of our self and subsequently turn that image into fact. What our real capabilties are we cannot be sure. Therefore the self-doubt, fear, and discouragement that often assail us must be overcome, so that we are free to pursue our destiny and self-development without those millstones dragging us down.

Consequently we need ways to deal with any negative mental habits that we possess so as not to succumb to our fearful fictions.

EXORCISING THE DEMONS OF DOUBT

Your weak points have no true value to you. You can only build on your strengths. You can prevent or lessen your weaknesses, perhaps, but you can't constructively build on them. That's why negative feelings you have about your weaknesses are not useful. Consequently, don't give them credence or strength. Do not build their strength or reality by worry, doubt or other negative thoughts or feelings. Stop feeding your weak points; starve them to nonexistence. Don't focus on them at all.

You might ask, "How can this be?" All of our lives we've been told that criticism can be constructive, even self-criticism, and that our weak points are things that we can and must compensate for.

Your weaknesses are weaknesses, and that's all. Unfortunately, by dwelling on them we enhance them. We feed them, we build them and we become, in effect, weak. Let's stop that nonsense once and for all.

If you have a weak voice, begin breathing deeper to give yourself greater resonance. Try other techniques as well. Then as your voice and speaking style become stronger, think and talk about "my voice is becoming stronger" *not* "my voice is weak."

It is therapeutic to get your negative factors and the bad feelings associated with them out into the open. We build our fears if we don't deal with them openly. Get them out where you can look at them and see if they are real. Then ask yourself, "What are the causes of each of my weaknesses? Do I dwell on these weaknesses because other people have told me I'm weak; because of my past experience; because of situations where my weakness has been exposed?" Whenever these negative thoughts arise and you recall a weakness, say to yourself, "That's not like me!" and thereby deny sustenance to your deficiencies. When you've exposed them, use these items as an action list for self-development.

If you tend to stammer, practice pacing yourself and use visual aids to relieve the tension on your memory. If your appearance detracts from your presentations, decide what you can do to improve it. Whatever the weakness, an antidote is available.

Before each meeting ask yourself, "What is the worst thing that could happen during this specific meeting?" Since that meeting is the only thing you can take care of at that time. Then ask yourself, "What kind of feelings am I experiencing?" Then ask yourself three questions about each negative feeling: (1) Am I exaggerating? (2) Is this feeling related to reality? and (3) What can I do to overcome this feeling?

The important thing about our fears is not to deny their existence, but to use them as planning "starter points" so that we can handle contingencies as they arise. Develop a checklist of things you can address to ensure that virtually nothing goes wrong. Each fear or potential disaster can signal a planning opportunity. As your options for overcoming problems increase, your anxieties will decrease.

As you realistically assess your risks, ask yourself if you can live with them. If the risks are still too high, you may want to consider what is your best alternative to giving this presentation. Unless you expect actual violence, you will probably be better off taking your chances on addressing your audience. Only you can decide, but that decision should be based on realism, not fantasy.

A hostile audience can be an opportunity as well as a risk. It can give you a chance to stretch yourself a little—to grow in your skills and experience. Don't pass up such an opportunity lightly.

Going with your strengths rather than lamenting your weaknesses makes a lot of sense, because only your strengths can give you success. Compensating for weakness only brings you up to ground zero. After you pass ground zero you need to be dealing with a strength, and our strengths can be built upon.

Demosthenes, regarded by Plutarch as the most eloquent of public speakers of that golden age of orators, started with a speech defect and a weak voice. But he could speak. Building on that, he practiced his speeches at the seashore, challenging the roar of the waves. It is also said that he put pebbles in his mouth so that he would have to speak slowly and clearly. He recognized his problems, but devised ways to overcome them. He also visualized himself as a great speaker and worked hard at perfecting his art. His rewards were substantial—as yours can be.

By rejecting our negative self-programming habits we can strengthen our self-image, prepare ourselves for greater future success and rid ourselves of those demons of doubt and despair that make our lives unnecessarily wretched and dismal before we even begin the encounter with a difficult audience. In the next chapter we will deal with how to turn negative messages into positive ones and prepare ourselves for more productive encounters in the future.

CHAPTER NINE

Getting yourself in shape to handle a tough audience

Within our human limits we tend to become what we think we are. There is also considerable evidence that we can alter our self-image by feeding positive messages to ourselves and that this new *programming* can alter our subconscious behavior in a myriad of positive ways. Since our subconscious mind tends to accept what is said by ourselves and others in the present tense as literally true, we need to ensure that past weaknesses do not dominate our future. The negative list that I offered for your examination in the previous chapter demonstrates that we can run into a *mental bind* if we aren't careful. We tend to speak of the past as though it is our future and in this way defeat ourselves. We tend to talk about what was the case as though it is true at this moment and will be true forever after. This is nonsense, but it is a way in which we reinforce the negative beliefs that we have about ourselves.

For instance, at the top of the negative list that I gave as a sample, is: "I get nervous." A closer statement of reality is that "I have gotten nervous in the past." What difference does it make how we word it? The answer is important. In the "I get nervous" statement, getting nervous is projected into the future and my mind will accept that as my current and future reality. It implies that "I get nervous *whenever*

I meet a difficult audience." In reality getting nervous is something that has been the case in the past, but it is not necessarily going to be the case in the future. We tend to talk about the deficiencies we've displayed as if they are true and will be true forever and ever.

We should remember that we are programming our subconscious when we recite the past as though it is the present and the future. This is why we may not change for the better even when we greatly want to change. If you insist on talking about your deficiencies, talk about them as though they are truly in your past.

Later in this chapter I offer some suggestions on how to overcome this "nervousness," how to become more relaxed, and consequently more effective with your presentations. If you say: "I get nervous," you are reducing the possibility of making these relaxation techniques effective. This business of language and how we use it is critical. Let's look at some other examples.

"I stumble over some of my points." That indicates that in the future you will do the same. The only thing that you truly know for sure is that you have done so in the past.

"I don't handle questions well," is another example. What we can say is that "until now I haven't handled questions well," and even that may not be actually true. It is more likely that "sometimes I haven't handled questions well," or, "I haven't handled some kind of questions well." If I develop new answering techniques, but still believe in my mind's eye that I don't handle questions well, the chances are good that I'm *still* not going to handle questions well in the future.

"I stammer" should be stated "I have stammered." "My stomach aches" translates to "My stomach has ached." "I get angry when challenged" might better be "I have gotten angry when challenged." What we're doing is avoiding letting the past dominate the future. By casting such statements in the past we are posing them as problems to be solved and are making it difficult for our subconscious to accept them as reality.

This kind of exercise is not just a game. Most people constantly tell themselves things that are negative and consequently come to believe them. Eventually these negative things become true behavior.

Stop using these negative descriptions of yourself. You can tell your subconscious more positive things about yourself and make it believe these more positive attributes. Consequently you can change your future by not assuming that your past is prologue.

When you start changing some of the things on your negative list from the present into the past tense, ask yourself, "What do I hear myself saying in rebuttal?" When you go down the list and change a statement from "My stomach aches," to "My stomach has ached," what do you hear your inner self saying about that—"that this is nonsense?" that, "My stomach will always ache?" that "I'm made that way?" Sadly, we often imprison ourselves in negative past belief when we can change any of these aspects with enough resolution and work.

When you hear yourself making these negative rebuttals, write, several times, positive statements that will replace the negative statements, such as: instead of "I sometimes stammer," say:

"My voice is clear and controlled."
"I have complete mastery of myself and my words."

You may want to create a new list where you translate past weaknesses into positive affirmations, for example:

PAST WEAKNESSES	POSITIVE AFFIRMATIONS
I have stammered.	My voice is clear and controlled.
I have gotten angry when I've been challenged.	I am calm, cool and collected when challenged.
I have stumbled over some of my points.	My points are made accurately and with dispatch.

You can convert negative past weaknesses into current positive affirmations by choosing antonyms for your deficiencies and building them into a positive statement about yourself. Repeat these positive affirmations to yourself whenever you are concerned about some negative aspect of working with difficult groups. Realize that you are a developable human being and can change virtually everything about you that you are determined to change—if you want it badly enough.

Central to all of this is the issue of transferring negative thoughts into positive ones. You can overcome things that have been drawbacks in the past and not let your liabilities master you.

ENHANCING YOUR POWER

Your positive list is what you have going for you and it may be quite a bit. Add to these items positive things that people say about you, successes that you remember, and your positive attributes that other folks have recognized. We all have something to offer and usually it is a lot or we would not have the opportunity to deal with a difficult audience.

Build a stronger positive self-image by concentrating on your attributes as strengths that can help you through difficult situations. Begin a new internal dialogue with yourself that is positively oriented and that will prepare you to better battle the demons of doubt wherever or whenever you encounter them. Use *everything* practical that you've got going for you to maximize your results.

Structure your presentation to capitalize on your particular strengths; build on your personal power. There is *no one way* to make a presentation. Make it authentically yours by focusing on those strengths, those positive things that *you* have to offer. Realistically appraising your attributes and maximizing your strengths can enhance your self-image and consequently your future performance.

Speakers and presenters do best when they are calm, cool and collected, yet looking forward to their time on stage with pleasurable excitement—relaxed, yet confident and eager to face the challenge. There are a variety of ways to achieve this positive state including the relaxation techniques suggested below.

FOCUSED AWARENESS

Sit quietly in a chair in a private place. Have your back fully supported and your feet flat on the floor. You should be comfortable but not reclining (else you might fall asleep). Remove eye glasses or contact lenses and loosen any tight clothing, if you can. Close your eyes and slowly take three deep breaths, breathing in through your nose and out through your nose and mouth. Visualize your scalp and the top of your head. Imagine all of the stress and strain as flowing downward from your scalp and hair, leaving them very relaxed. Repeat to yourself several times, "All of the strain is flowing down, flowing down through my body, leaving the top of my head, my scalp, my hair, completely relaxed, completely relaxed, completely relaxed." Then mentally move downward through your body pausing at your forehead, eyes, nose, mouth, ears, cheeks, jaws and chin, and so on, until you cover your torso, arms, hands, legs and feet. At each point repeat the statement about the stress and strain flowing down, leaving your body completely relaxed, until you picture the tension and strain dripping off the ends of your fingers and toes. If extraneous thoughts enter your mind, do not fight them; leave them alone and draw your mind gently back to the exercise. When finished, count from one to five, opening your eyes on the count of three and stretching and achieving full alertness at the count of five.

Don't be surprised if there was a pleasant tingling sensation in your limbs, or a feeling of warmth, for if successful, your subconscious mind was relaxing your whole body. This type of focused awareness is a healthy state. This state of relaxation can relax you and refresh you so that you experience greater energy and alertness.

If during this exercise negative memories float to the surface of your mind, don't fight them, for that strengthens them. Just allow these negative thoughts to flow through your mind as you gently bring your mind back to more positive events and thoughts. This exercise—really a form of meditation and relaxation—should be effortless. Do not concentrate, for that requires effort. Simply remember that if thoughts that are extraneous to the exercise occur, lead your mind back to positive things and let the other thoughts wash away.

Another version of focused awareness, which is used just for relaxation and energy release, substitutes a pleasant remembered scene for your positive mental images. Here, you visualize the location and develop specific details for your mental picture. For instance, you might use a memory of an ocean beach. Once this picture is in mind, visualize the wash of the waves as they sweep upon the beach, the soft hiss of the surf, the shifting of the pebbles at your feet and the small birds that hop from place to place. As the details become clearer your relaxation increases and your cares recede.

A third version which accomplishes the same thing is to close your eyes and breathe through your nose regularly and evenly to become conscious of the sound of the air as it passes through your nostrils. Do this for about three minutes and you will find that you are far more relaxed than when you started.

These three methods of relaxing are just samples of the many other techniques that achieve the same purposes. All can calm you and help you prepare for interacting effectively with your audience.

USING POSITIVE MENTAL REHEARSAL AND PSYCHOLOGICAL REINFORCEMENT

A rapidly growing number of top-flight athletes are using a combination of meditative relaxation techniques and positive mental rehearsal to attain *consistent* top-flight performance. The meditative techniques are similar to those described above but these athletes visualize themselves as playing a flawless game, performing at their peak and winning handsomely. They also visualize the rewards associated with their accomplishments. The more of their senses that they can get involved in this mental construction, the more successful the exercise and the more likely are to be their achievements. Thus they recreate the sounds, the smells, and "feel" of a good game, including the joys of winning and the sense of accomplishment when they are rewarded. With sufficient mental practice their subconscious organizes their bodies and their minds to play a top-notch game.

This meditative approach has been found to be far more long-lasting and effective than exhorting or psyching players up for each game. Besides, these exercises relax the players and give them renewed energy when needed most.

In a similar way, participants in my training seminars report increased effectiveness: in making their presentations; in fielding tough questions; and in managing problems on the floor, when they use such techniques before they mount the podium. I know it works well for me. Try it—you'll like it! The focused awareness exercise coupled with positive mental rehearsal can be done daily. This usually requires about five to fifteen minutes, depending on how elaborate the images you want to create will be.

Here is one exercise to try. Think back to events in your life where you have been successful and gained other people's praise for your work—especially in the realm of speaking or talking to groups. Visualize them as vividly as you can. See the people, the events, your surroundings, as clearly as possible. Go through as many of the events as you can in the time you have, but don't hurry. Savor the feelings these scenes gave you, especially the good feelings you experienced at that time. When you are through or have used up the time allotted slowly open your eyes. In time you can use this positive recall to strengthen your positive self-image if you allow it to. If you keep replaying your achievements and good feelings, instead of remembering and dwelling on negative garbage, you can enhance your self-confidence—a precursor to any success.

One of the most powerful techniques to use when in this meditative state is to feed yourself the *positive* new information about yourself such as we developed earlier when we were converting our deficiencies to positive affirmations. If you repeat positive, healthy statements to your subconscious while deeply relaxed, these messages can form new habits. This can easily be done by preparing a cassette tape recording where you record your relaxation exercise and then add your positive statements about yourself. Play this recording every day for a month or more and if done well, you will begin to feel more positive about yourself and gain a better self-image. However, make sure your messages are truly healthy and positive—not an easy task for many people who tend to focus on the negative aspects of life.

If you go through the steps outlined above to get yourself in shape to handle a difficult audience and develop such skills to a high level, you'll be "Ready for the Ring," when your turn comes.

CHAPTER TEN

Launching
your presentation

Launching a speech on a hostile sea of faces is much like launching a ship. Newsreels have recorded graceful looking ships sliding down the ways only to go belly up on reaching the water. You may remember presentations that have gone the same way.

Ensuring a successful launch is not an easy job. It involves not only designing and building a well-structured workable presentation, but a lot of careful interaction in the auditorium and elsewhere before the craft hits the waves (of discontent).

A ship launching is: a publicity event; a social event; a last minute check of the operation of the launch; a ceremony; a christening; and a moment of truth as the craft slides toward the water. In this chapter we are going to discuss the planning of your event, which includes social interaction before your speech, the ceremonies and your first moves. All of these things are important to getting your presentation off to a good start, especially if the audience will be a negative or hostile one. We can never guarantee that the launch day will be sunny. However, good planning and an awareness of our opportunities can be helpful in ensuring a successful voyage.

ADVANCE WORK

When a launch is planned, a shipyard normally wants publicity, documentation of the event, selected visitors, a good send-off speech and assurance that technically all goes well. In launching a carefully prepared presentation we want at least some of the same things. We need good advanced billing, we want to ensure that the right people are there. We want whatever good feelings can be generated. We want to guard against technical flaws or interferences. And we want things to get off to a good start. Much of this depends on the advance work we do.

When the meeting date is set you should already have some things in place, in order to avoid late notices, slipshod communications and the appearance of incompetence. You should prepare your audience in the most positive way possible. The quality of your advance billing, in posters, fliers, news articles, letters of introduction and information packets, all project your image and can help your audience to accept you. Last minute panic or rushing about not only causes mistakes but costs you the opportunities inherent in well thought out and systematic advance work. All of this, if it is done well, will give you that helpful confidence that comes from being well prepared.

The meeting invitations (rather than notices) can give you a chance to establish your credentials and your expertise before the group ever meets you. However, many people are afraid to issue "invitations" because then people may not come. However, the softness of an "invitation" can be adequately handled in the body of the letter. The tone of the communication is critical, for it conveys much of your personality and attitude, so much that you as a person and as a presenter are likely to be judged by it. Careful planning of these preliminary contacts can maximize good will before you even begin your presentation.

The tone and content of the messages you send your audience should not be casually chosen or left to chance. All too often not enough thought goes into these communications or they occur spontaneously.

Where the audience may be hostile and you need their acceptance or cooperation, minute details become critical.

CONTINGENCY PLANNING

Alternatives are also critical. What if the meeting is out of town and you can't get there? What if your plane is late? Or your overhead slides are in your luggage and it disappears? Who is available to cover for you? Are they prepped on what to do, or do they panic and blow their explanations to the audience? Does your potential replacement, or the person who will cancel the meeting, have a viable plan and scenario to follow if you don't show, get sick or are so late the meeting must be cancelled?

Several years ago I was giving a series of talks in upstate New York in mid-winter. Scheduling problems meant that I could not arrive until 10:30 p.m. the night before, on a hedge-hopping commuter airline. If that flight was cancelled, the earliest arrival was 8:00 a.m. the next day. The audience was not expected to be hostile but they were "uptight" about being away from their desks for so long and during an administrative changeover. Their bosses, however, thought the meeting was important.

The coordinator and I set up a plan to ensure that we could keep in touch with each other. A bad weather contingency plan was given to each participant. The coordinator and I also worked out an alternative meeting schedule whereby he would launch the meeting if I had not arrived by 9:10 a.m. He would also reschedule events to have the participants do a small group study exercise if I was not in sight by 9:30. If I was not there by 10:30 or if the coordinator had received word earlier that I would not make it, he was to set a new date for the meeting and dismiss the group as early as possible. The participants could tell what type of weather they were having. With their anxieties relieved that they would not spend their day idly waiting for the speaker, they were generally tolerant of whatever occurred. In twelve meetings only one was postponed and in three the coordinator began the meeting before I got there. Because we had a solid contingency plan no resentment built up. Our visible preliminary planning showed that we were sensitive to their concerns.

Begin as soon as possible to establish rapport with your audience. How many bridges you can build before a meeting depends on how much time there is between your arrival, the start of the meeting, and on how many other demands there are on your time. However, the number of contacts need not be great if you want to grasp the mood of the group, or develop a few friendly faces you can look at from time to time for tension relief. In smaller groups, you can often meet a sizable proportion of their membership. The payoffs in lessened tension and hostility (toward you, not necessarily toward your issue) can be substantial.

"But I'm not a greeter!" you might protest, "I don't like doing that!" This, may be true, but what if you were hosting a party? Would you feel comfortable greeting people then, even strangers, and saying a few words to them? "Of course," you could reply, "but then they are my guests." Isn't that true of this situation also? Didn't they come to hear you? "But these people don't like me, or at least, they don't like what I'm about to say." The latter may well be true, the former is unlikely unless you've met before. However, a lot of people have a hard time separating the person from the issue that stands between you. This is all the more reason why we should get to know some of them personally.

The second protest I hear is that "it would seem artificial or phony." If it seems so to you, you might very well appear phony to them and your cause would be hurt more by your efforts to be friendly than it would be helped. People who feel comfortable meeting strangers usually have good feelings about themselves and about what they are doing, and their behavior shows it. Those who pump hands for their own selfish purposes also usually show it, for their feelings about the other person are often condescending and about themselves inadequate. By being artificially outgoing they hope to compensate for their perceived shortcomings. If you don't feel good about yourself and/or what you are doing, you might want to analyze that fact for your future benefit. Negative feelings about yourself or discomfort about interacting with others are very personal things. But beware of the possibility that you too are mixing your feelings about yourself with your feelings about the message you bring. Unless you are doing something underhanded or despicable, don't confuse the media with the message.

There is one more thing about making early contact with members of your audience and that is that people have a legitimate and human need for attention, recognition and acknowledgment, even you.

People tend to feel negative about folks who bypass them, turn away or ignore them. Such behaviors deny them their rightful recognition. A few minutes of interacting in a positive way with members of your audience can put a pleasant glow on the faces of many, otherwise "turned off" people. This positive behavior on your part can continue throughout your presentation with smiles and eye contact.

But, especially when you are dealing with a negative or potentially hostile audience, your most critical function is to establish the highest level of good will and trust possible before the meeting starts.

An incredible number of speakers see their job as only presenting their speech, and assume that if they do that well, things will come out as well as they possibly could. Consequently, they greet the meeting coordinator and are introduced to those who are favorably inclined toward them. They then chat with "pro" people, who are not hostile, then dive into a chair at the head table, stare at the ceiling and make small talk with whoever happens to sit next to them.

People who want to *affect* a hostile audience, however, regard this time as found money and use it to build bridges between themselves and their protagonists. The issue is how to approach an individual or group that they perceive as threatening? How do they sincerely say they are glad to see someone that they really wish had fallen down a well on their way to the meeting? These things are not easy. But personal attention to some of your audience early in the game *can* alter their perceptions of you and of the situation. Such efforts to extend yourself can keep your mind off your vague intimations of disaster and remind you that they too, are only people. If you run into expressions of anger or snide remarks, simply acknowledge them, focus inwardly on your positive mental rehearsal and realize that that person will at least have had a chance to "say their piece" and they are less likely to be quite so hostile from then on. If they seek to influence you, trap you or get a commitment from you during these preliminaries, smile and say something such as: "I'll think about that" or "we'll see."

Even if you are busy checking out your equipment, a smile, a nod, a handshake or a hello to newcomers can soften up the opposition and often make you feel better. However, if you want to convey a sense of power and authority these preliminary activities will detract from the sense of aloofness that you may want to convey. On the other hand, efforts to be outgoing will also make you appear more human, if that is your desire.

ASSESSING AUDIENCE MOODS AND CONCERNS

Making overtures to early arrivals has other pay-offs through checking out the reality of your pre-presentation audience assessment and filling your computer with "here and now" data that you may use to alter your approach. Listening especially to what people near you have to say can give you clues to their needs. Are they engaged in an "ain't it awful" exercise? Are they interacting as old friends or as strangers? If they are discussing the issue under consideration, how hot or excited, optimistic or pessimistic do they sound? Do they seem to be shielding their thoughts and feelings from you? Such "data" may give you ideas or allow you to do things to structure support within the group.

Experienced presenters have a large repertoire of ways to change audience moods and behaviors and get the group to take a new tack toward solving the problem. The issues then are: Should I innovate at this point? Should I get the audience involved in some activity that will relieve tensions? Should I try to catch their interest by diverting it? How can I impact on this audience early in the meeting or before it starts? Should I? What can I do to also *test* the mood and feelings of the group?

You may want to encourage some of the early arrivals to move up front. This can tell you a lot about the feelings of the group, and yet may help somewhat to break up patterns of participant interaction that were based originally on attendees seeking out their friends or acquaintances to sit with. It may also encourage a closeness in the group and a greater willingness to comply with your next request.

There are also a lot of ice breakers, that you can use early to ease tension. Clergymen and other speakers increasingly ask groups to hold hands with their neighbors while they sing a song, or to say hello to the person next to them to get acquainted. Though this makes a lot of people somewhat uncomfortable, they often will see you as an authority figure and probably will comply. In general, people seem to like this, and it can get the audience relaxed and prepared to interact more positively. However, if you try this sort of thing with a truly hostile audience you had better be good at getting compliance. If it bombs you might decide to talk about why they feel so uncomfortable, but since that can easily get you off the track, it is probably better to simply say, "All right" and go on with your presentation.

After your arrival, and as the audience troops in, you can also assess their overall mood, their concerns and their informal relationships. Have they arrived with pitchforks and torches? What type of nonverbal signals is the group sending? What is the tone of their conversation? Who in the crowd is deferring to whom? Who are the informal leaders that others are gathering around? Which individuals are likely to be active in the discussion? Who sounds loud and opinionated? What seems to be their tolerance level? How close to the surface is their frustration or fear? These people are able to give you valuable general information without being aware of it. Listen to what those near you are saying. Are they discussing the ballgame or the issue at hand? Do they seem comfortable with themselves, each other, or with the situation in general?

In these and other ways you begin to "sense" the audience and you can structure at least some preliminary support within it and perhaps improve your *launch*.

BEING INTRODUCED

The credibility and behavior of the person who will be introducing you should be above reproach. A person the audience knows, can trust, and likes, can do wonders for you.

The person who introduces you should:

1. Avoid upstaging you. You are the main event and though the introducer's personality should show through in a positive way, the introduction

should be brief and primarily supportive of you. Pick that person carefully if you can.

2. Gain the confidence of the audience (and hopefully transfer some of it to you).

3. Explain the relevance of your presentation to the audience's concerns and interests.

4. Present your credentials, expertise and experience in such a way that it reflects favorably on your ability to do the job at hand.

5. *Highlight* the type of information about you that you want the audience to learn; and this highlighting should be used sparingly to accentuate your strengths.

Generally, a good introduction is a short one. A brief speech focuses the attention on you and sharpens the focus of what you are about to say. You should prepare it together, if possible, and both of you should feel good about the statements and details it will include. A preliminary run-through with you serving as the audience is often a good idea.

If you want to provide the text for the introduction make it brief and focused. Give it to the person early enough so that it can be personalized to their style. Let them know what you consider to be essential so that they can underline and highlight those key areas. If you want them to read an introduction you wrote, use a large print typewriter and give it to them on one or two 5″ × 8″ cards. Make it easy for your presenter.

It is often a matter of personal judgment as to whether the person who introduces you should offer personal information about you. Sometimes such personal data can help the people in your audience to identify with you and perhaps strengthen your image. Personal data makes you seem more human and less aloof. But such information should be used sparingly or it will distract from the principle purpose of your address.

At this point, your host, or introducer, is ready to send you on your way.

CHAPTER ELEVEN

Dealing effectively with audience emotions

The primary difference between a "regular" audience and one that is hostile or difficult, is not so much the difference in viewpoint or objectives between them and you, but the high level of negative feelings that those differences generate. Learning new ways to understand and deal with such feelings can help you to get improved results from the groups that you work with.

A hostile audience is an interested audience. You don't have to overcome apathy or passivity. Worried, anxious, or fearful people whom you might address, want escape and reassurance. The despairing seek hope. The bored want diversion and stimulation. The emotionally cold, hunger for warmth and comfort. People who comprise the negative or difficult audience that you might face, want feelings that are contrary to their current state. You can help them gain their desires.

Anger creates energy that can be directed toward constructive group goals. A worried or fearful group can be soothed and given purpose and direction. When discouragement or despair hangs heavy over a crowd, their spirits can be uplifted. When they are bored or preoccupied, you can titillate or entice. A difficult audience is a challenge, an opportunity. Your rewards can be commensurate with the degree of their alienation—the greater their disaffection, the greater your triumph, if you can bring them around.

When people are upset with you or with your position on an issue, you may not like what you are hearing, but at least those people are involved. Signs of resentment or anger show that there is energy, and if you help redirect that energy to positive ends, a net gain may result from your meeting.

For anyone who deals with a difficult group, an understanding of human emotions, and the ways in which they trigger responses within all of us, can not only provide understanding of a meeting's dynamics, but more importantly, give us insight into actions we can take to produce good results.

RAW FEELINGS

The study of our emotions and how they operate is far from complete, but even this partial knowledge can be helpful.

Some psychologists believe that there are four *primary* emotions and all the rest of what we call feelings (other than purely physical responses such as pain) are either variations of these or combinations of them. They are as follows:

1. *Fear*, which includes worry, apprehension, and anxiety.
2. *Anger*, which covers irritation, rage, resentment, exasperation, and ire.
3. *Grief*, which encompasses sadness, depression, anguish, woe, and bereavement.
4. *Joy*, which is expressed as happiness, gaiety, elation, and gladness.

Anger may not always be a true feeling, but instead a manufactured response. Some researchers call anger a secondary feeling, one that is used as a way to overcome the negative effects of fear or grief. Because excessive fear can immobilize a person, and excessive grief can lead to suicide, anger serves as a trigger to behavior that will take us beyond those two dangerous feelings. Therefore, when anger is defused or ventilated you can never be quite sure what will surface. Those emerging feelings (usually grief or fear) need to be dealt with effectively. In our meetings we need to ensure that we don't do things that unnecessarily trigger fear or despair, so that the audience generates anger as an antidote.

Each of these basic feelings can be visualized as a spectrum, running from the barely perceptible to an extreme which would be visible to all of us. Thus I can be "concerned" about a situation, you might be "worried," a third person might be "terrified" and a fourth person might be reduced to "a babbling wreck"—yet all of us are feeling fear.

Also, sometimes what we describe as a feeling, is actually a combination of an emotion and our physical response to that emotion, such as with hesitation (based on fear). Another might be excitement based on fear and joy (as in some types of sexual excitement).

There are also more complex combinations of feelings. When I was first introduced to the concept of the four basic feelings it made my efforts, to understand what another person was experiencing, a lot easier. However, there were a few feelings, such as guilt, and disappointment, that I could recognize, in myself and in others, but couldn't easily put into these four categories. I eventually came to recognize that disappointment was a subtle blend of grief, or sadness, and anger (with perhaps a touch of fear tossed in). Guilt I believe is founded on fear, but layered with sadness. Enthusiasm seems to be joyful excitement. Perhaps some of these feelings are more complex, but this insight is adequate for most of the practical purposes of dealing with feelings in an audience.

The four feelings listed above are *natural feelings* that everyone can experience in a broad spectrum throughout most of their life. However, we need to look at some special aspects of feelings and how they are processed.

ADAPTIVE FEELINGS

Some people are dominated by one kind of feeling, and their approach to almost any issue is affected by that feeling. Some folks feel depressed a good deal of the time. They will have a hard time getting excited about anything and may not show up at your meeting, even if they believe that the outcome would mean that your organization was going to dump radioactive wastes in their back yard. Others bristle and show hostility in virtually everything they do. In short, some people let one feeling dominate their personality. This probably comes as no surprise to you, but seldom do we relate their words, attitudes, or even their behavior to a specific dominant feeling.

Many (perhaps all) people learn early in life to modify (exaggerate or suppress, and so on) one or more of their natural feelings into what we call *adaptive feelings*, in order to survive in the environment in which they are raised. Some people learn that raising hell pays off in their home environment. These people tend to exaggerate anger whenever they encounter opposition, and take to shouting and threatening. They believe that people only pay attention to them (and perhaps will only meet their needs) when they create a commotion. They become wedded to the notion that raising hell is the *only* way to get things done. At this point the decision to raise hell is no longer a conscious one but has become a subsconscious habit.

Some other people learn that nothing they do will get them what they need, so what's the use of making a fuss—they learn to "go along." Their feelings of hopelessness and helplessness cause them to be passive. Most people fall somewhere along this spectrum with various degrees of assertiveness, or the lack of it. These *excessive* "feeling habits," that are often the source of trouble in an audience, are usually of such long standing that an individual is not even aware when their emotional response is inappropriate or counterproductive. Sometimes these feelings and their consequent responses can be confronted effectively, or perhaps we can demonstrate that they are not helpful in the present situation.

CONTROLLING FEELINGS

Only you and I can *control* our own feelings. One of the great illusions in life is the magic thinking that we can control another person's feelings. The notion that you can't comes as a shock to some, but certainly history and literature are replete with examples that show that you can't *make* somebody love you, though we seem to keep trying. In every case the other person does the choosing. The belief that others control our feelings is not only an avoidance of our responsibility, but robs us of the opportunity to fully master our own feelings and consequently to *influence* theirs successfully.

"He is always walking out of meetings and slamming doors behind him," describes his behavior, which we may want him to stop, but the slamming doors are symptomatic and don't get to the heart of the issue—which is his anger or frustration. We may want to confront this behavior, but it would also be helpful for him to release some of the anger that is triggering this behavior. It is possible, on some occasions, to provide the person with a chance to ventilate their feelings and so dispose, at least temporarily, of the consequent behavior. We'll discuss some ways of doing this later on, but we may have to identify and deal with their feelings before we can get them to change the behavior that is bothering us.

In a similar way our behavior may seem to scare the hell out of someone, but this isn't what is really going on. They sense that our behavior is threatening, and their mind locks on to the emotional and physical reaction that they (not you) consider appropriate, and then "choose," consciously or subconsciously, to get scared and to act scared. "But," you might counter, "even if I were to recognize some validity in this idea, what difference does it make? I yell and they jump—I get what I want."

Ah! There lies the problem. Since they control their reaction (even when they are reacting without thinking, out of habit) they always have the option of behaving differently than we expect. They can jump, but they can also get angry and lash out at you, or spend a lifetime getting even. Our behavior may *influence* another person by giving them options that they hadn't perceived before, and therefore they may *choose* to feel and act differently. This business of behaving in ways that allow our audience members to choose new and more productive responses, is the art of an effective speaker or meeting manager.

People can also choose to change some of their long-standing behavior patterns that are based on unthinking subconscious habits. This is happening more often, as people learn new ways to handle their negative feelings more effectively. As you meet more and more sophisticated audiences, don't be surprised if your old patterns of behavior no longer have the same effects they once had.

FEELINGS: OUR LOST RESOURCE

Feelings, good and bad, can be one of our primary tools for problem identification and problem solving. Feelings are an elusive resource that can power great events, or create enormous tragedies. Sadly, I must report that in training thousands of people to identify feelings that other people are experiencing, and then using those feelings as data for solving personal, interpersonal or group problems, I have consistently found that few people in any walk of life can clearly identify, articulate, or deal effectively with the feelings being expressed by another.

It isn't that people don't have the innate ability to read other people's feelings; but simply that this ability has been lost or trained out of them. So many people have learned to *suppress* their feelings and to *discount* the feelings of others, so that unless a person says to them directly, "I'm angry," they might not recognize the feeling. They are simply not very good at picking up, reading, and interpreting the non-verbal and verbal signals that are clues to another person's feelings.

We have been so shaped to listen for "facts" that we have forgotten how to hear the most important "facts of life"—our feelings. It is feelings that give life meaning, for to have no feelings is to be as dead. This concentration on "facts" has led many people to miss a large part of, or the key part of, *problem* messages. Especially they miss the nonverbal clues to the other person's feelings the tone of voice, body posture, and facial expressions, as well as the words chosen to express their feelings. We need to stop thinking of emotions in an audience as purely negative, for they can also serve as powerful motivators for goal achievement.

The more critical the level of feeling being expressed, the more insensitive or fearful we become to it. Most of this indifference, fearfulness, or inability to deal with feelings effectively is a social and cultural phenomenon that affects our Western society in particular. Although in our society (at least in the past) women generally have had greater permission to feel than men do, and consequently tend to be better at reading feelings, the one feeling that many women are taught not to deal with effectively is anger—usually the critical feeling when dealing with a difficult group.

These are generalizations to be sure, but they are generalizations that have been confirmed by research and observation. Though great differences exist among individuals in their capacity to read the feelings of others, as a group, we generally do a poor job of hearing and using feelings for productive ends.

DYNAMICS UNLEASHED

Feelings are drivers toward accomplishment. We don't want a feelingless audience if there is an issue to be dealt with, or a problem to be solved, that involves people. Feelings create power that we can use. But, if we want a powerful audience, how do we influence it?

A meeting on any controversial subject is like a power generator, so let us visualize your audience as a powerhouse where (hopefully) you are at the control panel. By going through the right procedures, and by using your judgment and creativity, you can channel the amount, direction and result of this energy flow; you can coax the power from the generators; you can provide the path it will take; you can direct the purposes it serves; you can feed it into other power networks; and, you can prevent overloads if your design and operation are right. As your power oscillates back and forth and builds in intensity, you can direct the surges of energy, dampen overload and feed the external power grids as required. We often don't want to reduce feelings, but to influence and direct them. When we interact with an audience, they detect our feelings as we detect theirs. Though we tend to focus on their emotions, ours are equally critical. As we work our emotional interchange together, the energy may spill over to those outside the meeting (the press, family members, the public at large, and so forth). Thus we can envision our powerhouse as a part of the larger grid in which we are operating—an emotional system.

A MODEL FOR INFLUENCING OUR AUDIENCE

It is most helpful if we do not try to judge our audience's feelings, but to accept the reality that emotionally they are where they are. With this view we are less likely to get upset or angry ourselves, and therefore more likely to do what is necessary to get them from where they are, to where we need them to be. This desired movement need not be manipulative—it can be honest and forthright if we are truly accepting of them, and aiming for as much of a win–win outcome as possible. We are much more likely to try to be manipulative if we ourselves have negative feelings about them, or about their emotional state.

The model of needs and motivation, illustrated in Figure 11–1 (adapted from Abraham H. Maslow's diagram based on a Hierarchy of Needs) gives us a way of looking at our audience and their feelings

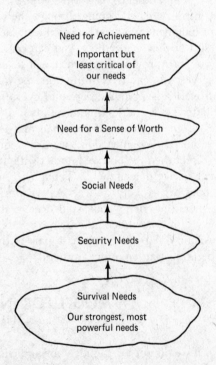

AUDIENCE NEEDS AND MOTIVATION

Need for Achievement

Important but least critical of our needs

Need for a Sense of Worth

Social Needs

Security Needs

Survival Needs

Our strongest, most powerful needs

FIGURE 11–1

that can provide an approach to developing win–win outcome and gaining the mutual satisfaction that comes from win–win.

When people's needs are not met they tend to react to that deprivation; when their needs are threatened, not surprisingly, they have strong emotions about that threat.

Because survival is our most powerful and pressing need it evokes our strongest emotions. When these food, clothing and shelter needs are seen as being at stake, we shouldn't be surprised if people get intensely upset. However, which emotion is felt and expressed depends upon the background of the individual. One person when faced with unemployment may be angry, another scared and a third depressed. In an audience all of these feelings may be occurring to different individuals at the same time, and any given person may change from one to the other as your meeting progresses. What you can be sure of, however, is that their feelings are intense.

However, this very diversity, while it may be hard to grasp, can provide us with a variety of ways to interact with a group. You may have some reassuring facts for some, a set of hopeful options for others, and perhaps a way to redirect the anger of the rest.

Generally, if a person can see the end of the threat to their survival needs, they tend to move to the next level of concern, which is their security needs. This is the assurance that they can hold on to what they have and that their survival needs will not be threatened in the future. This need for security exists in all of us, but, depending on our personal emotional history, we will carry it within us or perceive it as being safeguarded by membership in a group, by laws or by contracts.

Again, if a person can see the end of a threat to their security needs they will generally move up the ladder and become progressively more interested in meeting higher level needs. Thus it goes with each level of the model. As needs are reasonably well met we get interested in more complex but less pressing needs. Therefore some may leave your meeting, if they feel reassured that their survival and security needs are no longer threatened, while others may stay because they want to interact with the group, and thereby meet their social needs.

These social needs are expressed as our hunger for acceptance by others, a sense of belonging, as well as, love and friendship. Though membership in a group may also meet lower level needs (security and survival) it is a quite powerful basic need in itself. Our social needs can cause us to join others in violent protest or seek to make the group into a happy family.

However, when we feel secure enough in our social relationships, it is not uncommon to start thinking about the special contribution we can make to the group, or how we can gain recognition for ourselves. These *ego* or *esteem* needs, as they are often called, can motivate us to make helpful suggestions or to create a scene.

Finally, if a person is recognized as contributing to a group, they may try to lead it, or at least influence where the group is going. Therefore they may satisfy their sense of achievement—to really make a difference even if the direction of their influence is negative.

These last two motivators, a sense of worth and a feeling of achievement, are tricky. Although each of us has a need to think well of ourselves and to be well thought of by others—a sense of worth, this doesn't mean that our behavior will be objectively constructive. If our behavior confirms our self-image (or ego) or is endorsed by our peers (esteem) we can justify nearly anything. In a similar way, if the only way that we can see to achieve something is to block a motion on the floor, we may do so, even if it brings on a deadlock. It should be no surprise that some of the great triumphs and disasters of humankind have been brought on by people seeking to achieve obstructionist objectives to which they were powerfully dedicated.

However, for most people the further up this chain of motivation we go, the less intense the feelings tend to become. Therefore:

1. If we want to lessen the emotional tension in our audience we should, to the degree we can, avoid things that would threaten their needs, especially their lower level needs. We should strive to do what we can to meet these lower level needs so that they can move upward into less intense regions of motivation.
2. Recognize the diversity of feelings in your audience and focus on the things you can do to accentuate their positive feelings.
3. Provide appealing options that will help to move people up the chain, while feeling good about you and themselves.

For example, you might avoid a show of power which is likely to be seen as threatening to their security and survival needs, and consequently cause them to band together against you. Being frank about the scope of their problems may confirm their worst suspicions, but they will also not need to impress you with their concerns. Your honesty and understanding of their need to know what is going on may cause them to see you as more like them, even though issues divide you.

First, satisfying the lower level motivators just causes contentment and a sense of satisfaction—that is, an absence of pain, worry, helplessness or anger—they do not, in themselves, make us feel good.

Second, joy and enthusiasm are more likely to occur toward the upper end of the list. So if we need our audience to give us a positive outcome from our meeting, it is more likely to occur when people are involved, being recognized for their positive contribution and achieving healthy goals.

Help your audience to move up the chain in healthy, happy ways, and they will reward you.

Our emotions are a two–edged sword which cannot be denied. We can use feelings to blaze new trails of human understanding and cooperation, or they can spring back and wound us badly. Use this sword carefully and well.

CHAPTER TWELVE

Reading your audience from the platform

As we gaze over a new audience, be it large or small, we tend to see it "en masse"—a blend of faces without much individuality. Gradually we may begin to pick out individuals whose faces we like, or who seem friendly, or who tend to stand out in the crowd. Individuals emerge from the great blur slowly, if at all. We may sense great hostility in some, friendliness and acceptance in others, but the larger the crowd the more difficult it seems to identify people as persons. What speakers need is a way to observe an audience more closely, and to understand both group and members' behavior so that we can design more effective responses to difficulties that groups and their members are experiencing.

A SYSTEMS APPROACH TO UNDERSTANDING AUDIENCE DYNAMICS

Almost all the literature on public speaking and audience interaction tends to focus on either a mass approach to viewing people in groups or on reading individual "body language." However, the sociologists' interest in group dynamics offers us another viewpoint that I've found more useful in ferreting out concerns and problems which are obstructing achievement of your (and possibly their) objectives.

People come to a meeting for their own *primary* individual purposes, even if it is only to put in an appearance or to keep their boss off their back. Some want to be heard, others want to make sure that you don't put anything over on them.

However, on a *second* level they are trying to meet their personal needs within a group context. Within a short time most audience members are chatting with new or old acquaintances or glancing about the room trying to find someone with whom they can communicate. These relationships might be simple emotional bonds, "knowing that I am not alone," that "there is someone like me here," or "someone I know is here." Or they can be more substantial links, such as sitting with old friends or recognizing someone with whom they have shared common feelings or viewpoints before. Typically, these emotional or utilitarian links form an extremely complex set of interrelationships and interlinking subgroups. An individual may have emotional, social or philosophical ties with dozens of individuals and groups within a single room. That person may interact with, or serve as a member in any of those groups and still respond to other individuals on occasion. Dealing with an awesome array of interlinked groups or individuals seems overwhelming for many speakers, but this is often where the greatest opportunities exist for problem solving, if we develop an effective way to operate in this sociological morass.

At the *third* level is the collective summation of what is going on in the whole group. Here we can identify group leaders, pick up common themes and operate on a more generalized basis. Since participants in a meeting expect to be treated as a group, they will often behave in collective ways, even when to do so runs counter to their own personal or small group objectives and interests, as when a group votes on an issue and an individual loses but still participates. They often either assume that group cohesion is a higher value than getting their own needs met or that they are obligated to conform. The net effect is that the group often tends to act as a unit. The difficulty in dealing with problems only at the top or whole group level is that individuals or segments often go along with the overall group reluctantly and hold reservations that can lead to a lack of support if the overall group runs into trouble when implementing a solution. To operate at only the large group level often glosses over the fine points of a problem, lessens commitment on the part of some group members and tends to miss opportunities for high-quality solutions. If we become more sensitive to individuals and to the cliques and subgroups that have important roles to play in any large group decision, we can often design better answers for problem solving.

LOOKING AT INDIVIDUAL NEEDS

A difficult or hostile group is composed of a lot of individuals who have group related, unmet personal needs. Some may be met in a group context, others cannot. When I talk to audience members individually I find that, in addition to their own meeting agenda, they generally have seven primary personal group related concerns or issues that they are trying to resolve:

1. *Role and Status.* Why am I here? What do I have to contribute? Who am I in this meeting?
2. *Relationships.* Where do I fit in? What behavior is appropriate here?
3. *Goals.* What do I want from this meeting? Can the group help me to achieve my goals? If so, how?
4. *Influence.* How much influence can I exert? How much should I allow others to influence me?
5. *Trust.* How much trust can I risk? How can we build a higher level of trust?
6. *Closeness.* How close can we get to each other? How personal? What distance should I maintain from others?
7. *Control.* Who will control what we do? Will others try to control me? How much resistance should I exert if others try to gain control over me?

These issues are seldom discussed openly or even thought of in these explicit terms, but remarks, gestures, and nonverbal behavior from audience members exhibit these concerns. If you hear an expression such as: "Not on your life," it often conveys an effort to establish distance between you and them. A comment from the floor such as: "We're not getting anywhere," expresses a desire to resist control by you or to take the group action in another direction. "Watch out for that one," directed at another participant certainly indicates a low level of trust. Nonverbal messages such as changing seats or turning away from the speaker can be just as eloquent.

A participant's efforts to resolve these issues lead to a variety of behaviors that are usually quite visible to the speaker:

1. *Speaking out.* This can be done by nodding, gestures, making a statement, giving a catcall or walking out, as well as by a lot of other quite obvious actions. These are usually efforts to define who the person is and what they represent in the group.

2. *Becoming dependent.* Seeking someone they believe to be stronger or more articulate, and supporting and encouraging that person.

3. *Declaring their independence.* This can be done nonverbally by cutting off conversation, turning away from another person or by waving them off. Any resistance to someone in the group who represents authority is counterdependent behavior.

4. *Dominating.* Attempting to assert personal dominance over group members or perhaps even over the speaker. This attempt to get their own way is usually based on a negative opinion of the capabilities or intent of those whom they would dominate.

5. *Fighting.* Bickering, quarreling, casting aspersions on others, calling names and impugning other people's motives may deal with a variety of issues on the meeting agenda, but often are the results of the unresolved personal questions mentioned before, since they are seldom effective ways to resolve issues of substance. Fighting may reveal problems of trust, closeness, influence, control and personal position in the group rather than the substantive content of their chosen words. Thus, while someone is complaining loudly about a budget item, often the way they are going about it is the real message.

6. *Withdrawing.* People often become sullen, preoccupied with their own thoughts, or take an unscheduled break in order to avoid dealing with uncomfortable feelings they are experiencing. They psychologically or physically leave the group. In some cases they may be merely

responding to an urgent call of nature, but frequently it is because they feel uncomfortable with their role in the proceedings.

7. *Seeking supporters*. When people feel threatened by what is going on or disagree with the proceedings, they often intuitively seek out people who are also uncomfortable, and form an emotional subgroup. They also may do this when the part in the program that they are interested in has not yet begun or is completed—as a way of keeping occupied. Members of these groups support and even protect each other by providing mutually interesting conversation, telling jokes, playing "ain't it awful," or making snide remarks about the leadership or other group members.

That may be all well and good, you may say, but of what value is it to know about these individual personal needs and the behaviors people use to meet these needs on their own? I find several advantages to looking at group members' behavior that way:

First, you don't have to worry about the micro-clues to what each individual is experiencing, such as "body talk," and the rather specific personal signals a person is sending. These seven behaviors are far more overt and can be assessed across a whole group rather than counting how many people in your audience have their arms and legs crossed or how many are shrugging their shoulders.

Second, these behaviors are fairly easy to interpret and so is determining their cause. You can often bridge the gap between what is occurring in the meeting and the behavior of a number of people. For example, when several people are seconding the attack of a dissenter, they are probably feeling inadequate to attack by themselves and are seeking dependence on someone they perceive to be stronger or more articulate or more effective. In a similar fashion, when someone is attempting to assert dominance over the group, they usually feel that their goals are in jeopardy, they distrust the capability of others and fear control by others who they don't believe will meet their needs. Since these behaviors are clear we can get a good idea of how many people are affected, or interested, and that mass of people divides before our eyes into a manageable-sized issue or personally oriented groups.

Third, this kind of assessment gives us some handy guides as to what we can do to meet individual needs. For example, at a condominium association meeting a woman was virtually screaming, hurling insults at the chairperson and the board, stating their motives were dishonest and that the group was being railroaded into a condo fee increase for the board's selfish reasons. She was being egged on by a small, but very vocal, group, while in other parts of the room some people were weeping, her opponents were angry and giving catcalls and some people were leaving in an indignant huff.

The chairman perceived the major unmet needs and stated: "I'd appreciate it if the room would quiet down so that Mrs. ———, as leader of the loyal opposition, could be heard without shouting (role and status for her, and possible control for him). I am determined that all viewpoints will be given a fair hearing if I have to stay here all night (her goal of being heard would be met and he retains control and possibly opens up the group for greater trust). I'll also suggest that since none of us can really get inside another person's mind and determine their motivation that we stick to the facts of the case (trying to exercise influence in the group) and develop ways that we can work together toward a win–win resolution of this issue (striving for greater closeness)."

In this case one of the participants shouted: "Why should we listen to her? She never listens to anyone else." The chairman replied: "By listening to others we earn the right to be heard—I'll schedule you next if you'd like to speak" (thereby recognizing his need and trying to set up a procedure that would meet other people's needs and possibly smoothing over relationship problems. Thus we can pay attention to significant audience behaviors, understand the need (or needs) that is unmet and develop a quick and effective antidote.

THE WHOLE AUDIENCE

An audience is far more than a collection of individuals and their subgroups. The size of your overall group and how it is organized (arrangement of seating, variety of activities, etc.) has a great deal to do with how you will be able to read the group, appraise your problems with it and decide how to act to best meet your objectives. If you are working with a small audience you can give attention to individual problems and needs and influence the subgroups considerably. In a large group, no matter how good your scanner is, it will miss a lot of detail—possibly critical detail.

How much you can pick up on an audience's mood from the platform depends on the method of presentation; your state of energy, involvement and alertness; the number of people out there, and the diversity and complexity of their behaviors.

When planning your presentation consider the amount of scanning necessary. For instance, the use of an overhead projector often allows you to watch the audience while you develop points that are clearly visible to you on the slide. Also, small group work, with each group developing a report or an exercise where people share their experiences may give you a chance to pass among the groups and get a sense of their feelings and viewpoints.

The job of the speaker or presenter is to gather a myriad of clues and cues and synthesize them into an overall assessment that will permit flexible behavior and move the group toward goal achievement. This is largely an art, but competence in this art can be enhanced through a study of the principles of group dynamics and group communication.

CHAPTER THIRTEEN

Defusing
a tense situation

There are many ways to defuse tension but quite a few are dependent upon our individual personality. Spontaneous humor will often break the tension barrier but here we are dependent upon our personal repertoire of jokes, funny sayings, anecdotes, etc., as well as on our intuitive assessment of the situation. Being relaxed, confident and in control of ourselves and our responses is the best way to be prepared for these opportunities as they arise. However, there are ways to defuse a tense situation if we understand more about how tension arises and what we can do to lessen it.

Aloneness can be one of the most frightening experiences a human being can encounter. I don't mean those temporary retreats from human contact that we all seem to need from time to time. But it is no accident that "the most cruel and unusual punishment" that we can give a person is solitary confinement. Therefore, if a person is experiencing a deep feeling, and there is no way to communicate that feeling to other people, it is as though they were alone in the universe—wanting to scream into space but knowing that there is no one to hear them. In a meeting, when a person is experiencing a deep sense of fear or sadness or even anger and people are not taking notice of these feelings, there is a strong need to make someone notice and acknowledge those feelings so that they will not be alone with them. It should not surprise us that if we don't deal with those strong feelings, they will make their needs known in loud and undeniable ways.

This need to know that we are not alone, or at least to know that we can end this aloneness if we wish, is one of the most fundamental human needs. From birth each of us must know that if we cry out that we will be heard and our needs attended to. But additionally we need contact with other human beings, we need recognition and we need to belong. These are not trivial needs; they are core to our being part of human society. Audience emotions often run high, not only because of grievances, but because they see the speaker as cold or aloof or not willing to deal with them as needful human beings—they see the speaker as denying them their "strokes."

THE USE OF STROKES

"Positive strokes" can help defuse a bad situation. What are these so-called strokes, and how can we use them?

Years ago people who ran "foundling homes" realized that the babies they were caring for, despite attention to their basic survival needs for food, clothing and shelter, tended to die in high proportion to their numbers. After considerable thought and study, the adminis-trators realized that the only difference in treatment that these infants received in their foundling home from what they would probably have gotten if they were part of a normal family was close physical contact with another human being and tender, loving care. The foundlings were fed, clothed and sheltered but the busy staff seldom had time to pick up, fondle, caress, hold and "stroke" these children. When the procedures were changed to ensure that every child was physically "stroked" every day, the survival rate rose to the normal range. Strokes are a survival issue for all of us and not to be taken lightly by anyone. They should also not be used in a condescending or manipulative way.

There are three types of generally recognized strokes: positive strokes, negative strokes and phony strokes. When people meet our needs we get positive strokes and these strokes tend to make us feel good about ourselves and about other people. Negative strokes are hurtful things done to us, such as beatings, intimidation, denial of our physical and psychological needs, punishment and put-downs. Researchers have found that while these strokes hurt, negative strokes are better than no strokes since we can survive with negative strokes (even though they may twist our personality) whereas we might not survive with no strokes.

The relevance of strokes in dealing with a hostile audience is two-fold. *First*, that if a person doesn't get positive strokes, they'll figure out a way, creatively and even subconsciously, to get negative strokes. This accounts for much negative behavior in general and certainly for some dysfunctional audience behavior. *Second*, if they aren't used to getting positive strokes, they may feel awkward and embarrassed if you give some to them. Therefore, don't be surprised if people engage in self-defeating, negative behavior that gets them into trouble or "put-down." Remember, a negative stroke hurts, but it is better than no stroke at all. Also, if we offer a compliment or the hand of friendship and the other person puts you off or is embarrassed, don't be surprised or react negatively, he or she just may not know how to respond to a positive stroke. The stroke probably felt good but they didn't know how to accept it. In time, enough honest positive strokes might help the person's self-image, so keep it up whenever their discomfort is not too high.

The last type of stroke, the plastic, phony stroke is a problem because the effect of the stroke depends on the receiver. If you give a phony stroke and the receiver regards your effort as positive, they will probably feel good about it. If, however, you are sincere and give an honest positive stroke and the receiver perceives it as phony, they will see your effort as a negative stroke. "He (or she) is trying to con me." If the discount of your stroke is serious, you can confront their behavior and tell them how to feel about it. Otherwise, you can let it pass.

Though a child needs physical strokes as one grows up and interacts with people other than family members, the strokes become less often physical and more often recognition strokes. Nevertheless, we *all* need high quality strokes throughout our lives to remain healthy and happy. Recognition strokes are very important to all of us and should never be undervalued. The negative evaluation "All he wants is attention" is an insensitive "put-down."

Recognition strokes can make people feel okay and this is what we are offering meeting attendees when we smile, nod, or acknowledge them. When we say hello, shake hands or chat with them even for a minute, we are giving them a stroke and usually getting some in return. Some of these good feelings can last the evening or longer. Acknowledging and dealing with an issue that is significant to your audience is a way of providing positive strokes. An honest and mature recognition of other people's needs and feelings can go a long way toward defusing a poor situation at your meeting.

THE UTILITY OF FEELINGS

Emotions, that quick changing audience kaleidoscope, are vital spurs to accomplishment. We can't motivate without them. An emotionless audience is a drag—an excited audience is an involved audience. Only people who are experiencing substantial emotion will do much. We know this intellectually and yet when we are distressed by negative audience behavior we often wish emotions would go away. Such a response, no matter how fervently we might wish it, would not be truly helpful to us or to them—it would not make the problem that they are concerned with go away. Feelings are the core of morale, the soul of esprit de corps. We need these feelings for problem solving or for reaching our goals.

We dislike strong negative feelings in an audience partly because of our fear of the behavior it will provoke. Yet violence and other negative actions happen most often when people *perceive* that they have no other way to affect the situation.

Past unsuccessful efforts to get their needs met or bad treatment by authorities may cause people to believe that nothing can be done. Unless you have worked with this audience before and have been perceived as part of the control group they resent, they seldom have personal animosity toward you. You may be a symbol and a lightning rod.

If you are a lightning rod, most likely you will eventually get hit. That may be your principal function. If that is the case, trying to make the lightning go away, trying to deny it exists or dodging it, is not likely to work. If you are a lightning rod you need to recognize that when the dynamic charges collect sufficiently in the atmosphere they are going to seek a path or outlet. You can channel this energy, ground it or deflect it, but it is going to come!

Unfortunately the ways most of us have learned to deal with group feelings are not very productive.

I have found through experimentation that when anger, fear, or hopelessness are expressed in an audience most speakers respond in one of ten ways that are not helpful. We often try to:

1. Argue (and try to persuade them with logic)
2. Threaten
3. Preach or moralize to them
4. Advise them or tell them what they ought to do
5. Give them an order or command
6. Ridicule, shame or discount them
7. Distract or humor them out of it
8. Ignore them (and pass on to others)
9. Impugn their motives
10. Blame or critize them

It is hard for one speaker to respond in all the ways mentioned in one presentation, but some people manage it.

All of these responses to audience threats and challenges are negative, and most are likely to produce even more negative reactions than those behaviors that led originally to the use of one of these ten responses.

DEALING WITH AUDIENCE FEELINGS

Speakers often ask, "But what else can we do?" Generally the answer comes in one of five forms:

1. We can *confront the behavior directly.*
2. We can *launch a discussion* about what they are doing or saying and why they are doing or saying it.
3. We can *invite them to continue talking.*
4. We can *acknowledge their feelings* and then move on.
5. We can *actively listen.*

You may not like or feel comfortable with some of these possibilities, but each has much to recommend it as a way of solving emotionally charged problems in a group.

CONFRONTATION

Effective confrontation of another person's behavior is an art and unfortunately most of us have not been taught to do it well. Most people have learned to respond either with violence, distraction or with one of the ten unproductive ways outlined previously. To confront someone effectively requires that you think through *what they are doing, how it affects you* and *how you are feeling about their behavior.* Then we need to combine those three things into an effective message and send it. Confrontation that works means that we let the other person(s) know that we expect a change. However, to be really effective we do not have to tell them *how* to change. There is so much to confronting effectively in a group context that I've devoted a later chapter to developing this specific art.

LAUNCHING A DISCUSSION OF THEIR BEHAVIOR AND THE REASONS FOR IT

Suppose a member of the audience made a derogatory remark about you and your position on an issue that was accompanied by much head-nodding and shouts of approval from other members. Let's explore your possibilities:

• *In launching a discussion* about their behavior you might say, "I can understand our differences on this issue but I'm curious as to why you feel it is necessary to personally attack me at the same time." You are offering them a chance to separate you from the issue and are now talking about what they did rather than the issue. It exposes their negative behavior and separates it from the issue so that their action can be looked at by the group.

• Another example might be, to offer a description of what the group is doing that bothers you, for consideration. Supposing they are trying to drown out your speech. You might say to the whole audience: "It is evident that some people don't want you to hear the information I have to offer. Are the rest of you willing to accept that? I think that this issue of interruptions should be discussed. Would any of *the rest* of you care to make a comment?"

For many speakers the idea of opening up the forum to people on the floor may be frightening, or a sign of weakness. Actually, it takes a lot of self-confidence to try such an approach, a belief that you can really manage the meeting successfully no matter what turn it takes. However, if the behavior of some group elements is so disruptive or negative that your objectives are already in jeopardy, this approach may work.

When a person is emotionally charged up, he or she is *not thinking* much about what they are doing. Therefore the invitational approach gives them a chance to look at their negative behavior. This often reduces the annoyance because it calls upon them, and everyone else, to *think* about what is going on.

THE INVITATION TO CONTINUE TALKING

A person who is wrought up tends not to be very clear about what they are trying to say. Some people ramble or become almost incoherent when angry. One way to slow them down, get them to think about what they are saying and make their point clearer to everyone, is to say that you would like them to explain their views more fully. You are investing group time on an individual, but if you believe that this person is trying to express a feeling or thought that is shared by a significant portion of the group, the time may be well spent.

Your move has to be honest and based on some genuine lack of clarity or understanding. If it is, you will generally see a visible reduction in the intensity of the one talking and a general relaxation throughout the audience. Often the level of hysteria in that speaker's voice declines substantially. The person addressing the chair no longer feels alone or under pressure. Usually they will speak more slowly and distinctly and make an effort to clarify both their point and their feelings.

You, as the presenter, can continue to influence the group by encouraging the person, asking for further clarification when necessary, and restating their points in more general terms that the audience can identify with. Most often, when this process is going on, the level of emotion drops substantially, issues are clarified and the group moves toward problem solving. The audience also tends to feel a lot better about you. To do this well requires considerable skill, but that skill can be learned or improved upon. Importantly however, you have not abdicated your position as conductor of the meeting. If the person tries to seize control, that behavior can be confronted directly.

After the person has expressed their position, you can reassert control by saying, "Mr. Jackson, I believe that we all understand your position a lot better; we are now more able to take it into consideration. Thank you." If the person has explained their grievance or feeling reasonably well they will most often believe that they have been heard, understood and considered. You have accepted their position and emotions as legitimate without necessarily agreeing with them. You have probably defused a lot of negative audience feelings.

ACKNOWLEDGING THEIR FEELING AND THEN MOVING ON

Sometimes people just have a need to be heard. Once they have expressed an emotion or a problem and it is recognized by the other person, they no longer feel alone and their feeling is grounded. "I recognize your concern for your job, Mrs. Smith, and the terrible effects a job loss would have on you and your family. The issue before us is what can we do about that." Or, "Acknowledging that you are very angry, sir, I want to make sure that your feelings are taken into account as we move toward a solution to this problem." This approach does not discount the person, their feeling or the problem. Once their concern or problem is recognized they are often willing to move on.

ACTIVE LISTENING

We all know from personal experience, that when we have a problem (fact) that is bothering us (feeling), it feels good to have someone we can tell our troubles to. Though you may have been trained to "not bother other people with your problems," it is good to have a close friend, a confidant, perhaps a mate or lover to reveal your feelings to. Often we don't need advice or sympathy, we just need "a chance to talk it out."

As we talk in a free, accepting atmosphere our problem and what we should do about it often becomes clearer. We often find ourselves opening up even further and exploring depths of our feelings that we had not previously ventured into.

Thoughtful, concerned listening, provides strokes and allows us to discharge or ventilate our negative emotions. We generally feel relieved and more confident afterward if we personally control the process of letting loose. We usually think better and frequently find it easier to make decisions. Since a difficult audience is composed of individuals with shared problems, listening to group members express their feelings can be therapeutic for the whole group and can help them move to solving the problem.

Because this type of active, involved listening is difficult and requires considerable practice to be good at it, I've left it to the next chapter for further development.

CHAPTER FOURTEEN

The power of listening

Many speakers never listen, unless there is a question and answer session. A chairperson may listen, but often quite selectively. A meeting facilitator listens but generally only for facts. Many program presenters do not see listening as their responsibility. Yet, without listening to the signals as well as the words your audience is sending, you may be creating a communications gap that can be filled no other way.

When a group has had a tough problem to resolve where animosity and conflict abounded, yet they concluded the issue successfully and with good feelings, the participants are usually amazed. Few of those people that were most heavily involved could really describe the process that brought them to that happy state. Yet when asked what single thing the speaker or chairperson did that made them feel good about the proceedings, they were quite clear about that. The majority responded:

"He (or she) listened to our point of view and showed respect for our opinions."

Listening is a powerful tool for lowering tension in an audience, turning people around toward more positive feelings and behaviors and setting up a climate for problem solving. Effective listening is also an active ingredient in problem solving as that process continues. Unfortunately, listening is not a strong point in most of us, especially if we tend, as most speakers do, to be people who broadcast rather than receive.

POOR LISTENING SKILLS PREVAIL

Tragically, we get very little training in listening. Yet, we spend approximately half of our time listening to others, especially when we're not working on the platform.

Speakers tend to be poor listeners because:

- They see no need for it in their job, which is to present, not to listen.
- They are often in a hurry to get on with their presentation.
- Frequently they are not interested in what the participants are saying.
- They tend to listen only for facts—when feelings are the real motivators in solving problems between people.
- They sometimes tolerate distractions which make it difficult for them to hear what is going on when a participant is trying to communicate with them.
- They also, like most of us, tend to let personal prejudices or other thoughts interfere with the sender's message.
- They frequently miss points by trying to mentally rebut when another person attacks them rather than listening to what the person is really saying.
- They respond to personal attacks with a counter attack.
- They engage in stereotyping and therefore do not hear what the person is saying because they are filtering that presentation by what they expect to hear.

LISTENING SKILLS

However, we can train ourselves to be effective listeners and the results we get will amply reward us for our efforts.

When we are interacting with a belligerent individual who is expressing a group concern or feeling, we have an unparalleled opportunity to advance our cause through listening. To listen well takes control on our part and an acceptance of the other person. Not necessarily an acceptance of what she or he is saying, but a belief that they have a right to say it and from their point of view a good reason for saying it.

To develop this acceptance we need to recognize the reality of *problem ownership*. When a person yells from the floor that you are a blackguard of the worst sort, questions your legitimacy and suggests that your mother slept under the front porch, it may be a little difficult to realize that that person has a problem rather than you. Even if those charges were true, that person probably doesn't know it and so arguing with him or her will only convince everyone that the guess was correct.

You may be troubled by what was said, and you may want to confront, but the point here is that it was their problem, not yours, that led to the outburst. To be accepting we need to separate their problem from your problem.

If you can listen to their problem when they are being provocative, without getting hooked into an argument or fight, you have an excellent opportunity to ground or defuse the negative feelings they are experiencing.

When we begin to listen to another person's problem, however, we may encounter some serious difficulties. There are basically two different types of listening—passive (or relatively passive) listening and active or involved listening.

We all do passive listening fairly often. This type of listening comes in two kinds: *First,* silence—where you simply pause, maintain eye contact and let the other person talk while you absorb what they are saying. If the person is very emotional, this can be therapeutic for them because they'll often talk out much of their anger or fear. However, because you aren't responding they don't know whether or not you understood them and eventually that may bother them. Statements like, "Aren't you going to say anything?" or, "Don't just stand there like a dummy," are strong indications that the person finds mere silence to be unsatisfying. *Second,* "noncommittal acknowledgment" where you offer a variety of neutral responses to their talking is often found to be more satisfying. If you nod occasionally and interject "Oh," "unhuh," "I see," "Mn-humm" and "Really" on occasion, they usually feel you are being more responsive. However, they still don't know if you are understanding them and they may eventually become dissatisfied with the exchange.

ACTIVE LISTENING

The alternative form, active listening, is the most powerful way to defuse a tense situation that I know of. This is often technically called *reflective feedback*, or *mirroring*. It is also a most powerful and precise art. A person usually needs to do it quite well or not at all when dealing with a highly volatile or inflamed group. In less tense situations the skill level need not be as high. However, the more skillful you are, the more you will learn and the quicker that person that we are listening to (and possibly the group) will move toward getting a load off their chest.

There are basically three modes of this active or reflective feedback type of listening.

1. Paraphrasing the content of a message and feeding it back. This deals with the facts of the message rather than the feelings. It is summarizing what the other person has said, or communicating to them, "You're saying that we'll be three weeks late on this particular job and this will affect seven different departments adversely, making it impossible to achieve the due dates on the important XYZ project— is that correct?"

2. Observation of nonverbal actions. This is where you observe what the person is doing nonverbally and feed that back to them. For instance, "Jeff, you seem to be somewhat agitated this morning—I noticed that you've been clenching your fist fairly frequently and you're scowling a lot and speaking rather sharply to people. Do you care to discuss this?"

3. Reflective feedback. This involves feeding back both the emotional content of the message and the factual part of the message, with the most critical emphasis placed on the emotional content.

Reflective feedback or mirroring is taking the sender's whole message, including the feelings expressed or inferred and feeding them back to that person in your own words.

This third type of active listening can be a powerful tool for defusing anger (or other feelings), resolving group issues and building bridges to your audience. It demonstrates clearly that *you not only heard the person but that you understood them*—otherwise your feedback would be inaccurate. The total message, the fact that they are concerned about and the feeling they have about that fact, is important, for a reflection of both will convince the other person that they have been *understood*. It is only when you can mirror the subtleties of their feelings that they know that they have been truly understood.

Feelings give meaning to a problem. The facts may stimulate feelings but the feelings motivate. Feelings are the human parts of a message and the source of difficulties in groups. Hearing their feelings allows another person to ventilate or "ground" those emotions so that they are no longer dominated by them. Being able to hear those feelings tells the other person that you are sensitive and aware of them and their state. This helps them to feel good about you and builds their basis for greater trust and confidence in you. They perceive you as being concerned about them and accepting of their feelings.

USING REFLECTIVE FEEDBACK

Feelings and thoughts that are inside us can't be sent to another person directly. They have to be translated into words, expressions, body postures, gestures, tones of voice and other coded behaviors. The code, not the internal feeling or fact, is sent. The receiver picks up the code rather than the "real" content of the message. This code has to be decoded to be meaningful.

These codes are symbols rather than reality. They *represent* the things that we are feeling and thinking. The receiver has to translate your message into understanding and awareness. If the receiver is good at reading the sender's code, especially if common cultural, linguistic and expressive keys are shared, the transfer of meaning is likely to be good. However, if we don't share a common understanding of the words, expressions and behaviors that the other person uses, the meaning can be missed by a wide margin. Particularly if the receiver is not sensitive to how feelings are expressed and fails to pick up nonverbal signals, real understanding may hardly exist.

By reflecting the sender's message the receiver also has a chance to get further feedback from the sender on how well the sender's message has been understood. They'll often say, "Yes, that's right," or, "No— what I meant was . . . ." Consequently the reflective feedback response virtually guarantees full and effective communication—a rare commodity when dealing with a troubled audience.

An example of a reflective feedback exchange was observed at a public meeting in county government a short time ago: A woman rose to challenge the speaker—the county commissioner. She shook her finger at him, wagged her head, and tightened her jaw. "You stand there like a grinning possum, just daring us to take this to court, you conceited ass—well, you'll be sorry," she said. He fed back the following: "You see me as arrogant and overconfident and you're very angry about that, aren't you?"

"I sure as hell am—and you sure as hell are," she replied.

This may not have done much for his self-esteem, but he was accurate in his feedback, as she confirmed, so that he knew that he had heard her accurately even to reading the nonverbal anger that she was expressing. This exchange also gave her a chance to get her feelings and thoughts off her chest and be understood by the person that she was attacking.

Reflective feedback is difficult to do well. Most of us would have to listen more carefully than we are used to. We then have to think about the words we're going to use to send the message back to the sender, in a way that is both personal and clearly demonstrates that we have both heard and understood them.

In reflective feedback the original sender (the one with the problem) encodes the message in a variety of forms which are rather special to him or her. Their family background, the vocabulary that they commonly use, the way in which they communicate nonverbally, as well as all the feelings and thoughts that are currently going on within them, all go into the message to make it uniquely their own. Your capacity to decode and to reflect *their* message depends not only on common language but also the other social and cultural things that you either share with that person or which you understand about them.

When you have decoded as well as you can, you have an *approximation* of their feelings and thoughts. Therefore it is frequently not helpful to say to the person: "I know just how you're feeling." They will usually respond to this by either thinking or saying: "Baloney." This is because what they are feeling seems unique to them in that particular time and place and circumstance, and their feelings and thoughts are not readily available to you. However, if you don't try to convince them, and instead send back your version of their message including the feelings, the chances are good that they will recognize that you have indeed understood them or come close to it, for you have clearly demonstrated that capacity.

Your reflected responses should be varied and reflect your own personality and speech habits—those that you would normally use. There should be nothing artificial sounding about this. You'll have enough trouble with understanding what they are saying, so don't get fancy about it, just talk normally when feeding back. There are a wide variety of ways that you can phrase your response, all of which are essentially correct.

If you try to reflect the message that the other person is saying and you miss it, they seldom will get "turned off" by the mistake. They will frequently simply say "That's not exactly what I mean—what I mean is . . .," and they'll go ahead and explain their original intent. They will recognize, subconsciously or consciously, that you're trying to understand them and generally won't be negative. They will work with you because they want to be heard and understood.

BENEFITS FROM REFLECTIVE LISTENING

The positive rewards for reflective feedback are substantial. You will learn more about that person and what they're thinking and feeling by reflective feedback than you will learn in almost any other way. Interrogations tend to turn people off because they are often perceived as threatening. This reflective feedback, if done well, is nonthreatening—it is receptive, and it only deals with the message the other person has sent. Consequently, they will often develop a higher level of trust and confidence in you and share with you things that they might be hesitant to share otherwise.

Reflective feedback requires a high level of skill for the greatest payoffs. As a practical matter you may want to practice your active listening to gain these skills in relatively nonthreatening situations so that you develop the art before you get into critical meetings. You can do this when family members or friends have a problem and want to ventilate it, in order to gradually develop your skills. If people react negatively, there is a good chance that you have done something that they saw as manipulative or negative. Try to analyze what you did wrong, repair it, and the next time do it better.

HOW TO DO REFLECTIVE FEEDBACK

Typically, reflective feedback response consists of three separate parts. The *first* is what is often referred to as acknowledging problem ownership. This involves a variety of lead-ins, such as: "From your point of view it seems that . . . ," "From where I stand it seems that you're saying . . . ," "As you see it . . . ," and, "What I hear you saying is . . . ," "The impression I get is . . . ," and so on. A wide variety of lead-ins are available to us and you should vary your beginning.

The *second* part is actually the reflection of the emotions that the person is experiencing, such as: Worried about, concerned, irritated, annoyed, upset, fearful, scared, down, depressed, etc.

The *third* part is the object of their emotion—that is, the "fact" that they are concerned about.

An example of a full message might be: "You feel (lead-in) very concerned (feeling) that you won't be able to meet your condo fee payments (fact)—is that correct?" The checking out of the message ("is that correct?") is not always necessary. In fact, if you are reasonably sure of what they are saying, don't ask a question.

The key to effective reflective feedback is empathy, the hearing of the feelings that the other person is expressing and turning those feelings into your own words in order to feed them back.

There are a number of other guidelines. Reflective feedback can be interspersed with empathic grunts, that is, noncommittal acknowledgments of their feelings: "Ah ha," "Yeah," "I see," and that sort of thing. We can also use occasional silence, if they continue to talk without prompting. If they are interested in pursuing the subject and are going right along, let them flow. Just remain silent for a while. If it starts to slow down, feed back the last feeling that you heard them express and that will often get them going again.

WHY USE ACTIVE LISTENING?

Active listening has several powerful benefits, such as:

1. You can use it to gather data to correct the course of your meeting.
2. It shows people that you are interested in solving problems.
3. It shows acceptance of the speaker/participant and the views he or she represents.
4. It demonstrates respect for others.
5. It helps the sender to better define, and possibly solve, the problem.
6. It often provides insights and even new ideas.
7. It encourages the sender to be more open and honest, and to level more effectively with the speaker and with the other people in the room.
8. It promotes a friendlier problem solving atmosphere. Tensions are reduced and people tend to interact more freely.
9. It enables supporters of the sender to feel that their concerns are being listened to and dealt with.

WHEN TO USE ACTIVE LISTENING

There are a number of problems in active listening or reflective feedback. You should be careful in trying to use reflective feedback unless you:

- Have enough time.
- Really want to give them a chance to sound off.
- Feel accepting.
- Feel reasonably separate from their problem.
- Want to use it as a precursor to problem solving.

You should hestitate to use reflective feedback when you have something you want the person to do in the area under discussion, otherwise it is likely to be manipulative. You should also be careful that you don't use active listening when the person has a legitimate dependency. If they need your help, give it if you can. You should also avoid using reflective feedback when you just don't feel good enough about the other person to express nonverbal empathy. If you try it at those times you will often send a double message and someone will catch you at it.

Active listening should not be used to excess in a group situation if the time limits are starting to hurt your objectives. If time is not a problem, or if the reflecting helps your objectives, then considerable involved listening might be appropriate.

It is essential that you recognize when a person or group is through ventilating and ready to get on to other things. You are not running a therapy session. Active listening is a way of helping the group and yourself to resolve issues that divide you from them. It is a tool, not an answer.

Reflective feedback can be used throughout the problem solving process. Frequently new feelings surface as the group processes proceed, and as new feelings arise you can reflect them.

Reflective feedback may also be appropriate after we confront them about their unsatisfactory, negative, or impermissible behavior. Confronting what they are doing will often send feelings to a high level and you can then reflect their feelings back to them. This will tend to lessen the level of concern, anger or fear, that they are experiencing, and allow their feelings to come down to where they can get into a thinking mode and work on solving the problem.

Finally, under no circumstances, should you use reflective feedback for manipulation. This type of active listening involves *reflecting* their message only. If you try to use reflective feedback to influence them in a particular direction, you'll probably get caught at it. If you use the technique well, they will probably cure their own problem and reduce the anxieties, fears or anger, that are keeping you apart.

ERRORS TO AVOID

There are several types of common errors people make when they try to use reflective feedback techniques, such as:

Exaggerating or Diminishing Their Feelings   When we first attempt to use reflective feedback on a systematic and planned basis, we may exaggerate or diminish the sender's feelings. We sometimes exaggerate the other person's feelings, for our own purposes, or because we are over-enthusiastic in our efforts to help them.

We sometimes lessen or minimize their feelings when reflecting because we are afraid of their level of excitement or anger and are trying to calm the person down. This often doesn't work because it just tells them that we have missed the feeling part of their message and that we haven't really understood them. We may have caught the emotion but not at the level that they are experiencing it. Frequently they will increase the volume to make sure that next time we really understand them. Feedback should be accurate. "You *really* are *very* angry," expresses their genuine high level of feeling. This is important.

Adding or Omitting   When we add to the other person's message we are putting our own message in and are often being manipulative. We do this when we want them to behave in a particular way. Since they are working at a subconscious level they will often detect our efforts intuitively and may say, in effect, "That is *not* what I'm trying to say!" They may *sense* the effort to manipulate and get angry.

Omitting sometimes is ignoring material that they have given you that you want to disappear. However, in a complex message you may naturally lose some of their message. If they have four or five points that they make in a row you may only pick up on two or three of them. This causes people to *seem* to go in circles, that is, they keep coming back to the same subject more than once. But in reality, they are trying to express unresolved feelings that they need to ventilate. Very often in group activities the person just doesn't feel satisfied and consequently backtracks, perhaps a number of times, if you keep missing the message. Therefore if they seem to backtrack, search for the feeling that we have missed and which they are still sending.

Falling Behind or Leaping Ahead   When you are repeating previous feedback or going over old material you are falling behind them. Usually, if they had been heard in the first place they are finished with that material. Repeating what they said earlier is often irritating to them and counterproductive.

Leaping ahead is when you jump to conclusions about what they are going to say. If you assume that you know where they are going, you will often miss the point when a person turns the corner and brings up a new topic or feeling. Also it does not take into account the possibility that the person may have solved an emotional problem or made a decision by talking it out and therefore may want to move on to a new area.

Playing Shrink   Trying to deal with "why" the sender feels a particular way, while ignoring the real message they are sending, is analyzing. When you are analyzing you often say to the person, "You're doing this because . . .," or "You're just feeling sorry for yourself." This will hurt the relationship and frequently anger the sender. It is often a putdown and a roadblock to communicating. Analyzing the message has no place in reflective feedback, and yet people do it fairly often because of their own negative feelings about the sender or about how the sender is behaving.

Repeating the Words   When you do not hear the real message the sender wants you to hear you might repeat the *exact words* of the message, or deal only with the "facts" and not get to the underlying feeling. This the sender often finds irritating because you, the listener are missing their real point. This *parroting* is the most common flaw in reflective feedback—it is the one that occurs when the listener is doing a perfunctory reflective feedback and not really dealing with how the other person is feeling. Such repeating often leads the speaker to say: "Yeah, that's *just* what I said," as though they were experiencing a high level of irritation because you are feeding back their exact words. Try to avoid this error; put their feeling into your own words when feeding back their message. We should also avoid starting each feedback with the same lead-in because this sounds like parroting.

Being an effective active listener offers you one of the most powerful tools you'll ever find for defusing a tense situation, for learning more about your audience and their concerns and for moving a group on toward solving their problems.

CHAPTER FIFTEEN

Confronting dysfunctional audience behavior

At times you may need to *confront* things that individuals, groups, and possibly the whole audience are doing that harm the meeting's purpose or you as the speaker. You need to do this so well that you get what you need without producing negative side effects.

Individuals chatting when you are speaking, booing, throwing things, stomping their feet, walking in and out of the assembly hall and countless other irritating actions bother different people to different degrees. Some speakers just increase their volume and go on. Others get petulant and attack the perpetrators. Some, if it gets bad enough, just quit. How we respond to this negative behavior depends on: our personality; prior training; self-confidence; the size and variety of our repertoire of techniques for managing our audience; the seriousness with which we view the consequences of this meeting and even how we happen to feel on a particular day.

Generally I find that speakers commonly respond by:

1. Withdrawing (few do, or can afford to do this).
2. Ignoring the behavior as long as possible.
3. Sending indirect messages through sarcasm or humor.

4. Asking or telling people how to behave ("quiet down, please," and so on).
5. Confronting (this noise level is bothering me).

Some distractions in *any* negatively charged audience are virtually certain. When they reach a level that interferes with you or other audience members, what should you do about it?

Ideally the group should discipline its own members, leaving the speaker free to present his or her own case. Considering the lack of recognized group leaders (other than the speaker) and the passivity of people when in a group of strangers, it should not surprise us if the group does not discipline its members. Even when someone is distracting the whole group it is often left to the speaker to confront them. Many speakers therefore see this challenge as mostly a question of: "At what point, to what degree, and just how do I try to control or influence negative audience behavior?"

THE ISSUE OF CONTROL

In a very real sense, short of the use of physical force, you can't control anyone! Paradoxically however, if people believe that you can control them, they may allow themselves to be controlled. Realistically:

- You can command them and they can laugh at you.
- You can threaten them and they can taunt you.
- You can preach at them and they can ignore you.
- You can tell them how to behave and they can continue to do what they want.
- You can criticize or insult them and they can do the same to you.
- You can impugn their motives and they can mock you.
- You can ask questions and they can remain silent.
- You can try to distract them and they can pursue their own course relentlessly.
- You can punish them and they can get even (covertly).

Although it may be imperative to use physical force on rare occasions, it is generally one of the least effective ways to work with people. Some of the realities of control that we don't normally deal with are:

• *First*. Most people appropriately don't like being controlled by others because it runs counter to our survival instinct.

• *Second*. If a person is comfortable being controlled, it's because they are used to it, or, more likely, because being controlled by others relieves them from taking responsibility for their own behavior and for the outcome of events. Consequently they "go along," but if things go badly they often say, "What do you expect from me?" You need to ask yourself, "Is mere compliance or lack of responsibility what I really want to achieve?"

• *Third*. A person's willingness to accept control by another depends upon a high level of trust and confidence in the person or group imposing the control. Usually when an audience is antagonistic, this level of trust is absent.

• *Fourth*. Short of being overpowered by physical or psychological force, a person always decides whether or not to accept control by others. They may decide logically that going along is the best option available. However, they make the choices—not you. You can offer threats of punishment and the enticements of rewards, but only the other person can decide which is best for them. "But what difference does that make if I get what I want," you might protest. Well, if they are the ones who are deciding they always have the option of making other decisions as well. They may choose to engage in coping behaviors by becoming passive, forming alliances against you, foot-dragging, bad-mouthing you privately and sabotaging your efforts. You may achieve the appearance of victory and gain none of the substance.

• *Fifth*. Some people have decided long ago in their life to accept control from recognized power figures or institutions. You may gain what you perceive to be power over them just by being in charge. However, this giving over of control to others is frequently based on a long-standing feeling of *relative* insignificance or powerlessness. The feeling underlying this type of compliance is often hopelessness and despair—hardly the ingredients of high-level performance and achievement. If you want commitment and enthusiasm for your project or task, such people may not give it. Their self-image may be so low that they see themselves as observers rather than participants. They will dutifully do what they are told, but seldom contribute much initiative.

Tragically, many speakers consider that if they get even the mere appearance of compliance, that that is all that they can hope to achieve (an indication of powerlessness on their part). They also *fear* that if they don't control people and things, they won't get what they need. Therefore they focus on getting power and control and take their chances on getting what they really need.

Other speakers know that their results are highest if the people are dealing with control themselves and seek to achieve positive goals. When other group members are doing something harmful they try to inspire and motivate those people to behave better. They don't, however, try to reward people for a change of behavior, for rewards are only efforts to make control pleasurable. They try to get people to change their adverse behavior because "they" want to. If you subscribe to or are willing to consider this last approach a possibility, the issue comes down to: How do we *influence* individual or group behavior to be more positive?

ALTERNATIVES TO CONTROL

If we are going to influence other people to change their behavior we need to use a method that:

- is very likely to get the desired result;
- will not produce *negative side effects*
- will not hurt the other person or the group's self-esteem;
- will build their sense of self-worth through helping you or the other group members;
- will not harm your relationship with them; and,
- will likely strengthen your relationship.

There is no guarantee that the confrontation methods offered here will work in all cases, but they have a far greater record of success than the methods we most often use when we try to directly control people.

Each of these alternatives involves direct actions by you. These are:

1. *Take measures that are unlikely to offend your audience.* Set up guide ropes to influence the flow of people into an auditorium; create "smoking" and "no smoking" sections of the room beforehand and open a window to get some fresh air, assuming that this will not discomfort those near the window.

2. *Acknowledge a problem and invite them to help in solving it.* For instance, state that some members are sending you a message by dozing off and ask what can be done to make that less likely (assuming that the cause is not the dullness of your presentation). In this case you might suggest a stretch break and that is okay. But they'll respond best to suggestions they make, especially if activity on their part is required. You may also gain from their imagination and their knowledge of the group and the situation. Generally you should be more concerned with the results than how they are achieved (as long as their methods don't give you or other people in the group a serious problem). With a seriously disaffected group you may not want to make such an open-ended play—they may suggest that everybody go home and actually start to leave. However, they'll often make usable suggestions which heighten their sense of participation.

3. *Express concern for the needs of other group members.* This need not involve criticism. It may simply state an observed fact or the logical consequences of their actions on others. Statements such as: "With all the side conversations going on here I'm afraid that a lot of people who want to, aren't able to hear." "I'm noticing that a lot of long speeches from the floor are causing other people to show impatience."

4. *Expose the disrupters' hidden problems or concerns to public scrutiny.* This has to be done carefully since making a mistake can raise the level of rancor. Examples of this (when you are on firm ground) are: "I know that many of you have been sent to this meeting and some of you have other things you'd rather be doing. I'll do what I can to make this experience worthwhile." Or, "I notice strong signals that many of you are irritated and annoyed—do you want to talk about it?" Or, "I have a strong hunch that some of you would like to turn this into a bitch session about management. That may relieve your anger but it won't do much for your future. I'd like to get on to something that

may be more productive for you." (At that point you had better have something productive to get on to.)

Note: All of these four approaches are open-ended; they may surrender some control to others; and they concentrate on solving a problem. The situation may also be helped by reflective listening to what happens after your statement. All also tend to assume that other people can make a contribution to solving the problem. A fifth approach and one of the best—sending an "I" message, will be discussed in considerable detail in the next section.

THE "I" MESSAGE TECHNIQUE

"I" messages are direct, open-ended statements of fact about what a person is *doing* or has done that is causing you trouble. They identify or describe observable and verifiable behavior that can be recognized and noted by the group. It does not deal with assumptions, motives, or mind reading.

Ideally an "I" message should come from the center of your being as when you are personally attacked or when you are injured in some way by another person's actions—hence the term "I" message. However, as spokesperson you may be speaking for the whole assembly, a portion of the group, or for yourself personally. An "I" message is internal and personal as opposed to a "You" message which is laying criticism on them. An "I" message focuses on what is happening to you or to your group. It is an attempt to avoid the put-downs or insults often inherent in "You" messages.

The difference between an "I" message and a "You" message is not contingent on the use of the word "You" or "I," but on whether the message emanates from your person or attacks the other person. For example, a person keeps interrupting at your meeting making it difficult for you to talk and you reply:

1. "Joe, will you please keep quiet for a while, you're interrupting me constantly," or

2. "Joe, when I'm interrupted frequently it makes it difficult to keep to my points and to keep my mind on what I'm trying to say."

The latter statement focuses on yourself and how Joe's behavior is harming you. It doesn't tell Joe what to do (as does statement number 1, "keep quiet for a while"). Joe can therefore decide (to his own credit) how he will meet your needs (if he decides to) and he deserves your appreciation if he does change to help you. Because the "I" message does not embarrass Joe with an implied "fat head" message, "Will you please keep quiet for a while (you dodo)," it is far more likely to achieve a beneficial change of behavior on Joe's part. The "I" message doesn't generate the resentment or resistance that a "You" message does. Since the "I" message is based on the assumption that Joe, once confronted about his behavior and perceiving the effect it is having on you, will change his activity to something more agreeable, this method does not suffer from the contentions of control.

You may be skeptical of such an open-ended message because of your prior training related to the importance of controlling people. However, I and many others who have used this technique have found that in most cases the other person not only does what you ask, *in their own way* but actually feels good about doing so. To achieve that goal however we need to *design a good "I" message.*

DESIGNING AN "I" MESSAGE

Creating a good "I" message involves skill. People often think that they have delivered an "I" message when actually they have sent a disguised "You" message or a weak "I" message.

An "I" message usually consists of three parts:

• *First.* A neutral description of what the person is doing that is bothering you or the other group members, or is interfering with the meeting. This description should be journalistic in the sense that it is reporting what is true or apparent. It is not judgmental or blameful, that is:

There are a lot of side conversations going on . . .

When you push your way onto the speaker's platform . . .
When you accuse me of illegal action . . .

Each should be a simple statement of fact based on what the person or group has done, or is doing.

• *Second.* A statement of the *tangible effects* his, her, or their behavior is having on you or your audience, now or in the future. It is not enough that you disagree with the person or the group or want them to change— their behavior has to be hurting you or the group right now or be likely to do so in the future. Examples of these that add to (and correspond to) the three descriptions directly above are:

. . . and the noise level is making it hard for some people to hear and to participate . . .
. . . our meeting is being disrupted and you are making it difficult for me to carry out my responsibilities . . .
. . . you libel me and damage my credibility with the group . . .

In each we are describing the actual consequences of their behavior as it affects us or our audience now or in the future.

• *Third.* You express the emotion or feelings you are having about their behavior and its negative effects on you. Again we can tie this onto the three partial statements given above:

. . . and that worries me
. . . and I'm damned angry about it
. . . and that makes me furious

The level of emotion expressed and the statement of the precise feeling being experienced (fear, anger, sadness, regret, and so on) should be appropriate to their behavior and to the effect it is having or will have on you. You should not pussyfoot if you are feeling strongly about what they are doing. Neither should you exaggerate your feeling.

Each sample "I" message given above would be put together and delivered as a clear statement. For example, the first one would be:

> There are a lot of side conversations going on and the noise level is making it hard for some people to hear and to participate and that worries me.

The others would be handled in similar fashion. Remember, it is harder to argue with an "I" message because it focuses on you or your group and not on them. Consequently because you aren't likely to hurt their self-esteem there is less chance for resistance.

Developing and sending a good "I" message that gets results is a high art. To develop the skill you might practice writing out "I" messages for situations that you have encountered or for the negative types of behavior your audiences or their members have displayed in the past. You can then refine your messages until you have a satisfactory repertoire of "I" messages that you can shape to your needs on particular occasions. This prior practice will prepare you to respond spontaneously to their behavior during a meeting.

For instance, if you have a group that tends to overstay recesses, you can create an appropriate "I" message. "When it takes thirty minutes to get everyone back in the room, it causes our meeting to end later and idles those who are back on time, and that irritates me," might be an effective message for one situation. At another time your concern may be that latecomers are asking questions about matters that were discussed when you resumed the meeting at the agreed-upon time.

BENEFITS FROM USING "I" MESSAGES

I have been designing and using "I" messages with difficult groups for over a decade. I find that they come easier with practice and that I can now "shoot from the hip" with accuracy and effect. The principal benefits of sending a good "I" message are:

- I deal with observable reality that all those present can see, and not with attitudes and assumptions.
- I tend to be more frank and straightforward and they appreciate my candor.
- They learn more about how their actions affect the speaker, especially subtle things that are not always obvious.

- I feel better about having done something explicit about a bad situation.
- I often learn a lot more (through subsequent active listening and feedback) about what is going on in the group.
- The group often takes responsibility for effecting beneficial change and usually feels good about doing so.
- It often facilitates problem solving.
- It often improves future relationships because I seem more real and needful—a person who can be affected by what they do—not a robot or overlord.
- I often understand myself and the situation better, especially my feelings.
- I more often get my needs met and win through to my objectives.

WHEN AN "I" MESSAGE DOESN'T WORK

When an "I" message doesn't seem to produce the results you were hoping for, don't despair—at least not right away. Few people are used to receiving "I" messages and therefore may not initially know what to make of your communication. Most audience members are quite used to receiving the dummy messages inherent in "You" messages and being told what to do. To get a message that doesn't put them down and which is open-ended may confuse them. People often need time to absorb the message, think it through, decide what to do and then do it. Initial nonresponse may merely mean that they are thinking about what you said.

You may also have sent a faulty "I" message; the other person(s) may see little or no value in the relationship; or they have unmet needs that they think exceed your needs.

Your "I" message may be incomplete, weak or perceived as not relevant to the business at hand. Here the answer is to fix or strengthen your message. That may be difficult to do when an audience is hostile but to do so may be your only hope for reestablishing your position with the group. Remember a good "I" message clearly reflects the *behavior* that is causing you a problem stated in a neutral way. Their actions must really affect you adversely and your feelings must be authentic, appropriate and clearly stated. Look at each part of your message to see what could be enhanced or improved to make it more powerful and effective.

In a similar fashion where the audience doesn't care what you think or feel or considers you irrelevant to the proceedings, an "I" message may have no effect. Commonly, where there is a lot of hostility or resentment, the group may see the relationship as ended. In such cases you may need to confront them as a human being who deserves consideration as such rather than as a speaker.

Finally, if you perceive that they have needs that they believe outweigh the value of yours, such needs may have to be dealt with before you can proceed.

Where the needs of the group members run strongly counter to yours, you may need to apply the conflict resolution techniques discussed in a later chapter. But first you may want to send an "I" message and then listen carefully and completely to their response (including hearing the meaning of their nonverbal communication). Here the reflective feedback technique may be used to find out exactly what is troubling them and perhaps even help them move toward a resolution of their concerns.

Sometimes your confrontation may generate resentment—some people aren't used to being confronted, they perceive it as threatening or generally dislike anyone who makes a fuss about what they are up to. You may need to acknowledge their resentment and reflect it back to demonstrate that you have understood them. However, this should not take the form of an apology or of backing down if their conduct needed to be confronted. After acknowledging their feelings you may decide to let the issue pass, but they at least know that you took note of what they were doing and they may change their future actions to something more positive (including avoiding doing whatever led to the confrontation).

When there is a lot of hostility and resentment in a group, many speakers fear revealing themselves, which makes it hard to create a good "I" message. If you fear that the group wants to punish you, you may not want to let them know how their behavior is hurting you; they may say to themselves, "Good, let's keep it up" or even "That's great, let's increase the pressure." Their dream that, they win–you lose, may be a powerful incentive to continue to act up.

While some individuals and even whole groups may do just that, some of the other techniques that we've learned may be useful. At least the hostility is out in the open and you can acknowledge their response and get on with dealing with their problem of resentment.

I generally find that when the group makes an effort to punish the speaker, a good "I" message still produces better results than the alternatives available. Most people are more interested in solving the problem, if they believe that they can, than getting even—so use their strength to get on with it. If we use their strong feelings for our purposes we can usually manage the meeting well.

Sometimes the person who causes you a problem doesn't perceive or believe that their actions are adversely affecting you, and this lack of perception can be common to a group.

If you see that this could be the case and they do not change their behavior when confronted, and if hostility doesn't seem to be the cause you may need to send another, but different, "I" message. You might say, "I mentioned before that it bothered me that a lot of side conversations were going on, and because they are still continuing, I can only conclude that you aren't taking me seriously and that makes me very angry." In this case we are no longer talking about the side conversations but about the problem you have right now—ignoring your needs. In confronting behavior we should not nag—we should stay current with the new problem.

Shaping "I" messages to a group situation, confronting as soon as a behavior gets to be serious and creating an "I" message on the spot are not easy things to do. Practice and more practice is needed. The benefits of doing so successfully, however, can be abundant.

Confronting dominant group behavior especially is not easy, but if it is successful the group often changes what is necessary and this moves the meeting forward. We must recognize that people are not necessarily wrong, bad, or extremists because they disagree with us or are obstructing our progress. They have their own needs and concerns and want answers to their problems. If we *confront* the negative conduct that is flowing from those unmet needs and concerns and still acknowledge the possible legitimacy of their needs, we can move on toward problem solving. People do things, even negative things for their own good reasons. We need to help them get over their counter-productive actions—perhaps at first by bringing these to their attention.

We need to deal with negative conduct early so that it does not fester or grow to the point where more serious actions are needed.

A lot of people ignore negative group activity because they don't know how to confront successfully, or because previous efforts have turned out badly. The techniques offered here can enhance our interpersonal and group related skills to the point where effective confrontation can be the first step toward conflict resolution, improved relationships between the speaker and the group, and the attainment of your goals.

CHAPTER SIXTEEN

Turning anxiety and hostility into problem solving

Because of high levels of concern or anger in a group we may overlook the potential for getting our audience involved in solving the problem—or contributing to a solution. Similarly, a community that discovers seepage of a deadly or debilitating chemical into their ground water, or has workers suddenly unemployed by a company bankruptcy may be so shocked that they don't realize how much they can do themselves to lessen their problem.

If chemicals are already in their water, or the local factory has closed, getting upset in a public meeting about who's to blame may be therapeutic but it seldom does much to help resolve their problem. People may need to ventilate their feelings but sooner or later the real issue will arise: "What are we going to do about it?" If you are a spokesperson at such a meeting, whether you represent the "guilty" party, the community, the irate citizens, the union, or simply your own viewpoint, you can help focus the group's attention on problem solving—an opportunity that may never come again if you miss this chance.

Unfortunately in such emotionally charged situations many would-be leaders mistakenly think that they must produce a course of action that will solve the group's problem. This is what I call the heroic syndrome. Consequently they may feel inadequate and impotent if they don't have the magic answer and will be inclined to grab at overly simple solutions to a complex human problem such as, "Let's sue the S.O.B.'s." This may be a proper course and certainly emotionally satisfying, but it may also block further constructive thought and possibly not deal with people's more complex and immediate needs. Remember, movie heroes work from someone else's script where the script writer could make all things come out right.

"Leaders," have seen groups bicker endlessly without resolution. Many do not believe that a group can take charge of a problem, sort out its parts, and develop workable solutions unless a "leader" is in charge who makes the decisions.

This low opinion of the problem solving capacity of people in groups is often shared by many of those people in the audience. Consequently, such "leaders" often waste the creativity, imagination and knowledge of group members. They fail to harness the energy, concern and commitment of those most intimately affected by the problem and they tend to reinforce the passivity, feelings of individual helplessness and the silent rage that often afflicts those beset by a widely shared dilemma. The old cry, "Why doesn't somebody do something?" might better become, "What am *I* going to do?"

In hundreds of incidents I've seen groups function effectively in solving varied and complex personal, community and organizational problems. The difference between such successful groups and those that bicker endlessly is that those which succeed have a logical and creative method of grappling with their problems and a belief that such problems *can* be solved *by the group*.

Qualitatively such productive groups usually generate more realistic solutions. Morale zooms upward; people feel better about themselves and about the group; and often they learn far more about the problem and how to solve it than when someone else does their thinking for them. They also usually learn methods for tackling mutual problems in the future.

Here is a ten-step method I've used successfully numerous times to help groups solve problems. The last six steps are modern variations on traditional problem solving methods. All focus on group work in a meeting environment. When substantial conflict exists you may need to augment these techniques by conflict resolution methods—a subject we'll address later.

PREPARATIONS FOR GROUP PROBLEM SOLVING (STEPS 1 THROUGH 4)

Nothing much gets done unless people are really committed to pursuing the solution(s) chosen. When leaders present their ready-made solutions they seldom have any way of gauging whether the group is merely nodding assent because they have no alternatives or because they really believe the solution is the best possible one. If wrangling occurs over the leader's solution(s) it is frequently caused by unresolved questions or issues that the leader's proposal does not address adequately. Therefore questioning and discussion are appropriate. Unless dealt with successfully, such issues are likely to fester and decrease commitment to the plan. When this happens the leader may feel challenged and even abused, whereas they really asked for trouble by trying to solve a problem without involvement or commitment from their audience. People are less willing today to allow others to make decisions that affect them without their participation.

An effective meeting leader can do four things to get the group ready for problem solving.

Step 1. Define Your Role as Facilitator

You might do that by simply making a statement such as: "My role in this meeting should be that of helper in facilitating group problem solving." If the group is sophisticated in using group techniques, that may be sufficient. If you are unsure, or if the group is drawn from diverse parts of the community or has been brought together only by this current problem, you might offer more explanation such as:

- I believe that you, who are most affected by this problem, know best what is a workable solution—I'd like to draw on that knowledge.
- Your ideas and know-how are needed to develop the best possible set of

answers to this problem. I'd like to make sure that those ideas are brought forward in an encouraging environment that allows you to make the best use of your contributions.

• You and your families are being greatly affected by this problem. Your whole-hearted acceptance of whatever we decide here tonight is critical in making those decisions work. It is important that any reservations you have are worked out to our mutual satisfaction. I want to make sure that your point of view is considered to the greatest practical extent.

The foregoing do not represent a "con job" unless you do not believe that group problem solving is necessary, useful or practical. These statements offer a simple set of objectives to pursue and hint at the "mutual" problem solving methods you plan to use.

Step 2. Identify the Current Problem(s)

"Beastly Industries" has already announced that their plant in your town will be closed July 17th, or "Hemlock Root Chemical Company" has been dumping their sludge near your lovely canal and ground water system for twenty-five years before the effects of their depredations have been discovered. The problem at this point is that: you will soon have 1200 wage earners of your community out of work, or that the EPA has indicated that it is unsafe for 300 families to remain in their present dwellings.

Getting your audience to concentrate on the current problem or problems is important because their feelings are often focused on the past. There is no future in the past and fretting about what "used to be" or "what might have been" diverts energy and attention from the present and the future.

Identifying the consequent problems that can be dealt with *here* and *now* is an important service that you can offer to the group. Such problem *identification* can frequently be enhanced by dividing your audience into small groups and asking them to identify the various "aspects" of the *current problem* that need to be dealt with. Stress that, "At this point we are not to wrorry about solving these subproblems or discussing them in great depth—we'll do that later. For now we only need to identify the subproblems so that we can be sure we've dealt with them before the issue is considered resolved." Usually, fifteen to twenty minutes is enough time for these discussions.

It is important that the speaker circulate from group to group; to make contact, to ensure that someone is taking notes; that someone is designated as group reporter; and to answer procedural questions if these arise. Summarize the small group reports and print them on a flipchart or overhead slide for all to see. Or type and distribute the notes to all members at a later meeting. This common list then becomes an agenda for problem solving and a checklist for assuring that the problems are solved.

Step 3. Let Participants Vent Their Feelings

Your audience came together because they are involved in a problem of common concern. Before they can become effective problem solvers they may need to let go of some of the strong feelings that are hampering their logical processes and their creativity. If the group doesn't deal with their feelings they'll often keep those negative feelings around, hampering the problem solving throughout your meeting.

I've found three general approaches to having the group vent feelings:

1. Let them rant.
2. Encourage group noise.
3. Encourage emotional expression in small groups.

Variations in these approaches can be numerous and other approaches are possible.

Letting Them Rant   This means opening the meeting up to short statements of concern or anger that vocal group members want to express. This can be dangerous. Many speakers are unwilling to risk the possible loss of control inherent in this tactic. If you try it, some brief reflective feedback might be used to reestablish your position and allow the participants to know that they have been heard and understood.

Group Noise   When you are a problem-solving facilitator you can encourage the group to "get it off their chest" by leading a group boo or a shout of defiance such as: "Beastly Indutries can go to hell!"

or, "J. Quillington Pierpont can drink his own fouled-up water." This approach may also be risky if you get too cutesy. The group can think you are demeaning their feelings. However, if you carry it off well, it will often break the ice and even restore humor and perspective to the group.

Small Group Venting   One of the safest techniques is to separate your audience into small groups of three to six persons and ask them to share their concerns and feelings about what has happened and to concentrate on how they are affected by the problem. People who are passive in a large group will often speak up in a small group. Some people can more easily express anger in a small group and thereby encourage others to state their views. This can be therapeutic without the whole meeting room being filled with acrimony.

Your concern about using any of these tactics is to ensure that no one tries to take your meeting away from you. Whether you encourage venting or not is up to you. It can help, but you may consider it too risky.

Step 4. Get Agreement on the Ground Rules for Discussion

For problem solving, a group often needs a clearly understood set of behavioral guides to keep them from sinking into unproductive actions. For example, we will:

- Deal with issues rather than personalities.
- Avoid mind reading and attributing motives.
- Avoid taking positions, at least until the issue is thoroughly aired.
- Shoot for win–win solutions rather than win–lose.
- Use creative techniques to develop win–win solutions.
- Engage in no long speeches or posturing from the floor (or by the speakers).
- Focus on problem solving—not recriminations.
- Listen to each other.
- Not interrupt with loud noises or other distracting tactics.

These ground rules may seem like common courtesy. But as we all know, unless such behaviors are brought to the conscious awareness of the participants, in a distressed group this ordinary politeness is often violated.

GROUP PROBLEM SOLVING (STEPS 5 THROUGH 8)

A lot of negative behavior in a group results from not knowing where they are going nor how they are going to get there (not because people are naturally quarrelsome as some group leaders assume). However, it is then that a systematic problem solving approach is most useful, for it provides structure and a constructive sense of motion toward some goal or goals. The next four steps are also basic to the conflict resolution techniques that will be discussed in the next chapter.

Step 5. Define the Problem in Terms of Needs Rather Than Solutions

It has been said for a long time that "a problem well defined is half solved." Few groups clearly define precisely what it is that is troubling them. Group members often assume that everyone else sees the problem as they do and so few people check out their perceptions in a public forum. Is it any wonder then that they often squabble and bicker endlessly? Every member in a group need not agree on the definition of a problem but it is important that each member understand as well as possible what problem the other people in the group think they are working on. To keep the group from quibbling over words and to set the scene for problem solving we need to concentrate on end results.

It is also important to realize that problem identification (mentioned in Step 2) is not the same as problem definition. Identification usually deals with symptoms and is part of the process of discovery. Problem definition is a more rigorous activity and deals with determining how you would know the problem was solved.

Focus on Needs versus Solutions   People usually define their problems in terms of their solution rather than in terms of their needs. That is, in fact, so common that I often get blank or quizzical looks when I suggest defining a problem in terms of needs. Yet the key to effective problem solving is to deal with our needs rather than with our solutions.

Solutions spring quickly to mind. This is what we want: "Reopen the plant and put us back to work"; "Clean up the ground water and take all those poisonous chemicals elsewhere!" Often the other party can't or won't meet our solutions—but they might be able to meet our needs—or at least some of them. To understand the powerful differences between needs and solutions it is important to realize that needs are open-ended, they do not imply any particular thing that has to be done to meet your needs. Solutions on the other hand tell exactly what you want them to do and usually imply a certain way of doing it (your way). There may be several ways that I can meet your needs, but only one way I can meet your solution—that is—do what you want me to do. Step seven in the ten step approach deals with generating solutions to meet the group's needs. Here we are trying to define the problem and it is appropriate at this stage to keep all of our options open.

When we zero in on our solution we back the other party into a corner and they are almost forced to fight or surrender. They will usually try to impose their solutions on us, thereby making conflict inevitable. When we state our needs we invite them to work with us, for we have not told them what to do or how to do it.

I usually find the needs approach is difficult but most rewarding. It also provides a benchmark against which to measure success. And it gets people away from trying to sell "their solution" before the problem is fully defined.

Defining the Problem—Methods   A vital function of a group leader is to elicit from the group an explicit statement of the problem as they see it. There are two primary ways of doing this:

1. Define and Redefine. Here the leader asks for a statement of the problem from a volunteer in the audience and records that statement so that it is visible to all. Then the leader asks for any clarification or modification that is needed. As suggestions come in from the meeting members the chairperson refines the definition to bring it closer to a group consensus. If the overall problem has several aspects, or if the group is faced with multiple problems, each can be dealt with individually in the same fashion. If the overall problem is very complex it may be worthwhile to assign small groups to define each subitem and bring them forward for review by the larger group. The goal is to produce a clear statement or statements that the overall audience can largely agree on. This is easier to do when we concentrate on group needs.

2. Decide what Condition (or situation) would Prevail if the Problem were Solved. Some people do much better at visualizing an end result. Neither approach is inherently superior, it is just that some people find one approach easier than the other.

In the original situation that led to the write-up of the Beastly Industries case, people at first were given to proposing solutions (such as reopen the plant) but finally settled on a generic needs definition that said: "Have steady, long-term employment for the 1200 people laid off at the plant, at wages roughly comparable to what they were making before the plant closing." This definition focused on an end result and left the solution(s) wide open for any kind of creative endeavors that the group wanted to provide.

Step 6. Get the Facts

You want only those facts that are relevant to the problem. In the Beastly case, the precise number of those laid off; how many people will probably retire or leave the job market; the skills and experience of those still seeking employment, etc., would be useful in developing a community-wide plan. However, having too many facts can be constraining. You might end up knowing too many reasons why something won't work or having more data than you can make sense of. Overelaboration on the facts is likewise inappropriate. A recital of Beastly's past offenses against the community, would heighten resentment rather than facilitate problem solving. A balanced statement of the present problem with supporting data is usually all that is needed.

A factual survey of the (human, financial and material) resources available to solve the problem is often better here than a highly interpretive one. Sketchy facts may be better than detailed ones at this stage if gathering the latter causes delay. Don't let your facts get in the way of generating a wide variety of possible solutions (step 7). For instance, if people regard the community resources as meager, they will tend to quickly evaluate some solutions as "Too expensive" or say, "We can't afford that" without ever considering ways to increase community resources. The main point is *do not* over-elaborate or deal with contraints.

Step 7. Generate Possible Solution(s)

This step is the one where the group's abilities are most often displayed. However, it is important that these ground rules be observed:

1. No critical evaluation of ideas is to occur at this step. No one can say, "It won't work" or interpose other roadblocks to considering any idea proposed by a group member. Derisive laughter, ridicule, smart remarks and other negative responses are out. The chairperson may ask for clarification if an item is not understood but such discussion should be brief and no justification of an idea is required.
2. Idea stimulating techniques such as brainstorming should be used. This is a technique where group members are encouraged to contribute *any* idea that occurs to them and to build on the ideas of other participants. All ideas, no matter how wild, are welcome because they may have some merit or they may trigger other ideas that have merit.
3. *All* ideas proposed should be recorded for later consideration.

The recording of the possible solutions should be visible to all. When the flow of ideas slows down, ask the group if there are any variations or elaborations that they could make on the items displayed. This often leads to new avenues of thought and additional items for consideration.

In the original Beastly case the community considered (among other things):

- A Task Force of local leaders, to attract other employers to the community.
- Buying the local facility and running it themselves.
- Forming a partnership with Beastly to keep the plant operating.
- Attracting Federal and State Funds to retrain displaced workers.
- Establishing a fund to help former workers migrate to areas where jobs were more plentiful.
- Establishing several small firms composed of people with similar skills who could solicit business in neighboring communities and with the Federal government.

The process of systematic problem solving in small groups proved so satisfying that a number of people used it to solve their own personal problems related to their unemployment—they went into business for themselves and over half succeeded, some even coming to employ others in time. The important thing was that all ideas were generated without defensiveness and were recorded for later possible use. About two thirds of the ideas so developed were eventually used by someone.

Step 8. Select the Best Solution(s)

Though this is the step where we apply our critical and judgmental abilities, they don't have to be applied negatively. No one gains when people vie for the opportunity to "chew up" other people's ideas. Instead we should think: "Here's an idea (someone's precious brainchild), what can we do to make this idea work!"

When a person throws out an idea they see some connection between their thought and the problem. The connection might be a tenuous one, but it is there. It is important to explore that perceived connection and build on it, if at all possible. At least it should get a fair hearing.

We should be particularly sensitive to the use of absolutes such as, "That'll *never* work, *everybody* knows that . . .," and, "*Every time* someone goes off half cocked," etc., and negative putdown statements such as stereotyping and discounting a person or their ideas. Such unproductive behavior should be confronted. We want adult-to-adult transactions in the group rather than the parent–child relationships so characteristic of people who tend to be critical and judgmental.

We should also avoid the search for the *simple* great answer that will solve all the problems at hand. Such grandiose notions are seldom realistic. Complex problems seldom are amenable to simple or singular solutions. Seeking *the* solution can lead us to miss good opportunities to chew away at a problem until it falls of its own weight. If you get a miracle solution, run with it. But life is seldom so straightforward.

Also, we should not overlook the reality that *all* of the ideas may not relate to *all* of the people. An individual in the group may see in a list of solutions a possibility which applies to him or her and be willing and able to pursue that idea on their own. In the Beastly case, a toolmaker got an idea out of the group brainstorming that led him to buy the equipment he used to work on and set up a profitable business in his basement. In similar fashion, small self-help groups might form around an idea or group of ideas that are developed during the solution generating phase. Having a great variety of ideas to work with gives each person and subgroup a greater opportunity to get "a piece of the action." The more ideas available, the better the group's human resources are likely to be used.

IMPLEMENTING AND FOLLOWING UP (STEPS 9 AND 10)

A plan only has value when it is put into effect. Steps 9 and 10 are the first times in the process that you should begin to worry about the "how" of what you are trying to do. To concern yourself with the "how" before you generate *possible* solutions causes most people to miss opportunities. Because we often cannot conceive of how we are to achieve a goal at the same time that we are generating solutions or evaluating them, we often confuse ourselves with unnecessary details. Once we have picked *our best* solutions we are free to use our imagination to develop innovative ways of making them work.

Step 9. Implementing Solution(s)

Few complex group problems have a single answer. It is usually necessary to lay out a plan of implementing the best solutions, working from the most helpful toward the less productive items. Some things can be done almost immediately with little group effort expended. Also, many actions can be taken in parallel while others need to be sequenced.

One of the easiest systems for making a project plan is to convert each desired solution into an activity or a list of activities (action items) which are needed to implement that solution. Then each action item is transferred to a card (3" × 5" or 4" × 6"). These cards (for each solution or group of solutions) can then be laid on a table or on the floor in the most logical sequence for accomplishing each. As these sequences are laid out we should distinguish between dependent items and parallel (or independent) items. Dependent items are those which require some previous item to be completed before the next step can be taken. Independent or parallel items can be handled simultaneously. By transferring the information on these cards to a large sheet of paper and drawing connecting lines you can achieve a "network" planning diagram of your program.

We can also list on the card: Who is responsible for implementing the activity; estimates of how long the activity will take; and details on what will be done and when it will be done. If group resources are limited, priorities may have to be set and the sequencing of activities can be governed by those considerations.

Step 10. Monitor Progress, Follow-up, and Change if Helpful

Generally treat major solutions as you would treat meeting objectives. These items should have due dates and progress toward those dates should be monitored. This may mean that your problem solving meeting will spawn other meetings or that someone is put in charge of following up on any projects that result from your original meeting. It is important that your problem solving meeting not just give birth to statements of good intentions without real results. A common complaint from meeting participants is that "We agreed to a lot of things but nothing ever happened."

As a series of actions are undertaken by the group, that very action changes the situation for better or worse. Therefore, it may be necessary to make changes to keep the solutions current and oriented to the dynamic "real world" environment in which the group lives. Minor adjustments may be made fairly easily but if a major adjustment is required it may be necessary to go through the ten-step process all over again. But this time the problem may no longer be the one the group originally dealt with. The new problem may be "how do we solve the problem of implementing the program we've already agreed upon?"

We should also not see changing our original plan as a negative experience. It may well be that as the solutions are implemented new opportunities arise that can be taken advantage of without surrendering the original objectives. Problem solving in groups can be a complex but highly satisfying activity.

CHAPTER SEVENTEEN

Resolving conflict in groups

The roots of this conflict spanned centuries and reached back across the ocean to an obscure and backward area of the Carpathian Mountains. But here in this ethnic, blue-collar neighborhood in our industrial northeast, resentments and feuds that had been smoldering for decades burst forth in a fist fight in a church vestibule. The neighborhood quickly divided along the lines of a local schism, the outlines of which had lain beneath the surface since the church had been built early in this century.

The church was a proud structure; large and of stone. It had three, blue, onion-shaped domes of the Russian (or more exactly Ukrainian) style. The services resembled the Russian Orthodox liturgy but this eastern rite church had a tie to Rome. The church founders gathered together people who shared a common language but the numerous dialects reflected the historical, ethnic and cultural diversity given them by various conquerors throughout the ages.

This polycentric collection of parishioners resulted from the waves of immigration that rolled into this community from the early part of this century. Historically, parts of their homeland had been incorporated into six different nations, most recently into the Soviet Union.

On top of this ethnic diversity there were conflicts about liturgy, theology, and modernism (or ecumenism). Some of the parishioners were fifth generation attendees while others had arrived in the United States from Europe and Canada in the 1950's and 60's. The conflict finally crystallized between those who called themselves "Old Catholics" and the so-called "New Catholics," but arguments about the language that should be used in the service and the terms of "old" and "new" reflected attitude rather than an individual's age or tenure in the parish.

When a general meeting was finally called to address the conflict the "old" sat on one side of the room and the "new" sat on the other. But those who cast a pox on both groups brought folding chairs to the meeting and insisted on setting up shop in the middle aisle—thereby giving the fire marshal a fit.

Lest you think that this type of conflict is bizarre in a house of God, I've encountered over fifty such bitter struggles in churches, synagogues and even a mosque. These fights for power or reform which have sometimes reached the physical combat stage have included: Southern Baptist, Methodist, Lutheran, Roman Catholic, Episcopal, Pentecostal, Orthodox and Reformed Hebrew and two Moslem sects. Differences over religious practices and beliefs, as history well demonstrates, bring out more intense hostility than almost any other subject. However, this church group using standard conflict resolution techniques managed to resolve their differences and bring the whole group together for a productive, mutually satisfying future.

If you think about the way people behave when they are involved in a conflict, whether it is interpersonal or intergroup, they usually attempt to dominate or to surrender or leave if they believe that they can't get their way. If one person or group thinks they have any chance of winning, they will try every trick in the book to dominate the other side including the use of position, power, tradition, expertise, statistics, or anything else that they have going for them. If their power or position is not enough, they will resort to persuasion, cajoling, logical arguments, guilt or manipulation. Unfortunately, this often wastes time, energy and creative potential. It also may breed resentment, resistance and a lack of real interest in carrying out the agreement that the "winner(s)" often think(s) they have achieved. In the church group they faced the possibility of the "losers" leaving the church, competing for adherents and weakening the economic base of the institution.

To be *really* successful in resolving conflict in a group, you need to consider three aspects of how many (or most) people view conflict.

1. Some see conflict as harmful and destructive and to be avoided at all costs.
2. Most people perceive a conflict situation as an either/or proposition, either I win or you do; i.e., a win–lose proposition.
3. Many naively believe that imposed solutions are workable solutions even where a genuine conflict of needs exists.

For this church group, some of whom had experienced warfare, subjugation and persecution, including that of both Nazi and Communist armies, it seemed that only hurt and harm have come from conflict situations.

Also, generally in a conflict each person *knows* that what they want out of a conflict is "right" and "just" and therefore assume that anyone who is in conflict with them is trying to do them out of their just desserts. Hence, their opponents are bad, or at least behaving badly. In a group setting this often translates into "good folks" (who agree with me) and "bad folks" (who do not agree with me). Group leaders, speakers, etc., often succumb to this syndrome and only in their calmer moments will they accept that perhaps the other side (or person) has a point.

Because power and its use to get our way is so ingrained in our culture few people have any other model to draw on. Because conflict usually generates strong feelings, people seldom think very well and the only creativity that they use is emotionally based; an intuitive creativity that is focused on "giving the other person or group the shaft before they give it to me (or us)." The idea that both sides could benefit from the conflict seems to be rare.

If we are going to be truly effective in resolving group conflict successfully we need to apply the three basic concepts for developing win–win outcomes or agreements.

1. Conflict can be productive and beneficial for it broadens our understanding of a problem, provides us with new ideas and information, and can lead to cooperation and cohesiveness in the group, if effectively resolved.
2. By the use of all the group's creativity, innovative solutions to problems

can be found which better meet the needs of all parties and lead to win–win perceptions on all sides.

3. Win–win agreements better meet the needs of all parties involved and consequently there is seldom need for resistance or resentment and a reasonable level of trust, caring and good feelings generally ensues. True win–win problem solving generates agreements that are supported by all parties since everyone has a stake in making it work.

It wouldn't be surprising if you were to say, "That sounds good, and it might work between two people, but how do we do it in a group setting?" You already have a great deal of the answer to that in the methodology offered in the chapter on problem solving. The rest of it centers around dealing with conflicts of needs.

CONFLICTS OF NEEDS

People seem to have two problems when dealing with conflicts of needs. They confuse wants with needs and they have a hard time identifying and distinguishing their needs from their solutions. This confusion often arises from the problem of equating the "what" with the "how" of things. I may want you to stop smoking because the smoke bothers me. But it really doesn't matter to me if you smoke or not as long as the fumes do not get into the air I breathe. Therefore my *need* is to be free of the smoke you are generating. How that is done often doesn't matter as long as the method used does not create a new problem for me. Needs tend to be rather basic and fundamental while wants are often less critical and are frequently a perceived solution to a more basic need. "I want a million dollars," is often perceived as a solution to a dull, degrading job, a way to have a more interesting life, a path to long-term security and possibly a method of gaining prestige and social standing.

The truly powerful thing about focusing on needs rather than solutions is that there may be many ways to satisfy my needs while only one way (the million dollars) to satisfy my solution. In similar fashion, wants become thought stoppers and often lead to disillusionment when the want is satisfied but the more fundamental need remains untouched. If I want a million dollars, I'm likely to focus on that goal and as long as I'm making progress toward that amount I'm not likely to ask why I want it. However, if I were to ask how I could get an exciting job, a more interesting life, a path to lifelong security and greater prestige and social standing, the possibilities include success in almost any field that appeals to me. My answer may include solutions such as: a research scientist at a government agency, a TV weatherman, a talk show interviewer, an author, a trainer or a producer of TV documentaries. Your list of possible solutions could be at least equally long. You may still *want* your million dollars but you are not likely to find many people willing to give it to you and it might take a lot of time and energy and sacrifice to get it. However, you might be able to find a lot of people who'd be willing to *contribute* to fulfilling your more basic needs. They may know ways of helping you that will not mean any great loss or inconvenience to themselves.

SORTING OUT CONFLICT SITUATIONS

Conflicts can be good, bad, or neither, depending on how we handle them and the consequences that flow from them. When conflicts arise in a group setting there is a tendency to try to control or resolve them from the platform for fear that if we do not, groups or individuals on the floor will seize control or they will get out of hand and damage the meeting and its purposes. This top-down or bottom-up approach (from the audience) characterizes many failed meetings. In each type of outcome the loser's needs tend to be ignored and often their values are trampled upon. When the issue devolves to "Who's in charge here?" people resort to fighting, withdrawing, sabotage and other coping behavior. A more relevant question is, "What are we trying to do here?"

In the church conflict during the first meeting our consulting team asked the group to do three things:

1. Define the conflict in terms of their needs rather than their solutions.
2. Try to envision a win–win solution where everyone would come away from the conflict seeing themselves as winners, not in the sense of the others losing, but in terms of each participant getting their needs met.
3. Each group (including the middle of the roaders) appoint or elect three of their members to serve on a "Committee of Reconciliation and Church Progress."

The first two requests elicited some strange looks and a few questions about what we meant.

The parish priest, who had been well briefed, gave some samples to show distinctions between needs and solutions, such as:

- I need to avoid fist fights among parishioners.
- I need to prevent disruptions of the services.
- I need to keep people from feeling they must leave the church.
- I need to have the support of all parishioners.
- I need a complete and lasting resolution of this conflict.
- I need to have every parishioner happy and supportive of the final solutions.
- I need your creative and innovative solutions to these problems that will show love and consideration of our fellow human beings.

Solutions, he said, involve the specific things that each parishioner *wants* for themselves as their way to meet their needs. Needs are open-ended, solutions are closed-ended.

Because most of the participants had spent their lives dealing with win–lose propositions, the priest believed that most of the people at the meeting thought he was being unrealistic, but at least the seeds were planted.

The third request, however, had better luck. The church hall was made available to each group on a different night so that they could elect their three representatives. This brought the working group down to a manageable number. The priest informed the whole group that their representatives would have three functions:

1. To gather a statement of group needs from their constituents.
2. To explain and clarify these needs to the other committee members.
3. To report back to their group statements of the needs of the other groups for discussion purposes.

Then the priest lowered the boom on them by saying that he didn't want any of the groups to deal with their *positions*. He said that when people take positions in a conflict they often produce a type of excessive demand. They therefore retreat slowly if at all from those positions and expect something in return for every concession. This leads to bargaining and compromise. He said that bargaining wastes a lot of time and energy and that compromise, while sometimes helpful, is seldom creative and generally leads to people splitting the difference and settling for half loaves instead of applying their creativity and imagination to producing more bread for everyone. The rest of that meeting was spent discussing what it was that the priest was talking about. When people started to express their anger or viewpoint the priest and one of his assistants would attempt to get that anger or concern translated into a perceived group need. That night a lot of people left the meeting mumbling to themselves.

Within two weeks the committee had been selected and had met twice. At each meeting the group was intensively trained in win–win creative negotiating techniques and then such training was offered to each of the three groups. The training produced some cultural shock, a lot of disagreements about the practicability of the concept and a great deal of discussion about the nature of the other group's needs. The win–win approach did not go down easily with these groups, except for the middle of the roaders.

THE BASICS OF WIN–WIN CONFLICT RESOLUTION

To resolve intergroup conflict, to develop genuinely workable solutions that meet participant needs, and to garner the commitment to those solutions requires working together as equals—adult to adult—to generate mutually beneficial solutions. To do this successfully we need:

- a clear statement of the issues,
- a focus on needs versus solutions,
- some notion of what state or condition would exist if the problem were solved.

We should strive to genuinely believe that your needs are important while my needs are *equally* important. We must also resolve to avoid the use of power—for we can't get people to trust us if we use our power to get our way.

It is important to remember that first and foremost no one states a *position*, and the group(s) are discouraged from taking a position.

Once we take a position we have locked ourselves into a solution and this is unproductive. The taking of positions limits our creativity, leads to selling our ideas and often to bargaining which is usually time consuming and mean spirited.

It is generally productive to use the ten step problem solving process offered in the previous chapter and focus on steps 5 and 7: Define the problem in terms of need rather than solutions and generate a variety of possible solutions. These solutions collectively should meet the needs of all concerned.

When we define the needs of each "side" in terms of their *needs* and list these needs on flipcharts or a blackboard, there should be a separate list for each side of the conflict. This allows the groups that are in conflict, including the chairperson to work side by side facing the lists as mutual problem solvers rather than to psychologically be working "across the table" as opponents.

When this is done it is not uncommon to find each side looking at the other group's list of needs and responding to it. In general this is appropriate because if you and I are in conflict, you are best equipped to meet my needs and vice versa. If I could solve my own needs adequately and you could do likewise, we would have no need for the meeting.

Unfortunately compromising and bargaining—helpful as they may be at times—often lead to getting less than we might or giving up more than we have to. These approaches have historically led to a focus on becoming a better bargainer or developing a better compromise for our side. This is unfortunate because neither bargaining nor compromising are generally very creative. When we concentrate on getting the best of a bargain or giving up as little as possible we seldom explore options that are outside the narrow issues at hand. We concentrate on what we've got or hope to get from the other party and seldom see the possibility of making the pie, which is to be divided, large and more flavorful.

If we look creatively at your needs and mine, we are often free of all but the most basic constraints and can go anywhere our imaginations lead us. In a group setting where a lot of people can contribute their ideas and expertise this is a remarkably productive methodology. Since ideas often trigger other ideas, we can all grow and develop together as we think of new ways to meet each other's needs.

In the church example, as consultants, we did training; did a lot of listening and reflective feedback and encouraged group members to ventilate their frustrations within their own groups in a Christian context without making threats or judgments about others. Group members learned to focus on their own feelings and actions rather than on what other people were doing or saying.

Finally, each group was led through a series of creative problem solving exercises, first by themselves and finally as a whole parish. The outcome was two Masses each Sunday—one for the "old" Catholics and one for the "new" Catholics using different liturgies, languages and rituals. Each six months the times of the Masses would rotate so that no one had to get up earlier or stay later all the time. Several other adjustments in policy and procedure were introduced, such as: a particular parishioner or family could attend either service and could select which one they attended each week; i.e., no restrictions were imposed on anyone except by the size of the church. The main burden for change fell upon the parish priest who had to prepare for two quite different services each Sunday, but he preferred the extra work to continuation of the conflict. As a result the congregation raised his salary, offered more lay participation in the service and arranged for more vacation time for the priest.

Not only did these and other diverse "solutions" meet the needs of all the parishioners, the group came up with several creative ideas that reduced operating costs, allowed the congregation to grow and improved church service programs for both the very young and the very old. This included tape recordings of each Mass for shut-ins and more ethnic cultural experiences for the children.

Today that church is a robust, harmonious institution that has an intense, renewed sense of mission and is very involved in outreach programs and contributing to the rich ethnic diversity of their community. In less than a year they went from a loser church to a model for their faith.

When this process of conflict resolution and creative negotiation is successful, we often find that we don't have to settle for half loaves of compromise or the competitiveness of bargaining. Communities that were filled with strife, and employees angry with arbitrary and insensitive management, have often been brought closer together through the use of such creative conflict resolving techniques. These are techniques that move an audience toward harmony and the settlement of problems.

You have to make sure that what the group and its members decide to do is clearly understood, that the level of commitment to the solutions chosen is high and that they have a method for adjustment if conditions change as the plan is implemented. The chairperson or people designated as responsible for monitoring such results may need to make the agreement explicit and resolve outstanding issues, check out the degree of commitment rendered by each party and ensure that they have the where-with-all and the mechanisms needed to ensure a mutually satisfactory result.

Although the process of creative conflict resolution produces good feelings among the participants, the success of such a resolved conflict—the actual carrying out of the win–win agreement by the participants, builds belief in the method and trust in each other. This is a road to real win–win conflict resolution.

CHAPTER EIGHTEEN

Stimulating a cold
or indifferent gathering

"What do you do when you get absolutely no response—nothing! You tell a joke and it just lies there—flat and dead. They don't even snicker," asked a young aspiring politician.

"M'lad," I said in my most fatherly tone, "that's their response. They couldn't have been more eloquent if they had walked out on you.

"If they've heard you, an audience always responds—even if it is by giving you nothing. Withholding can be one of the most powerful ways that an audience can deal with a speaker, and perhaps, to speakers, the most disconcerting. When the group as a whole is being passive/aggressive, fearful, preoccupied, bored, or feeling helpless and hopeless, there are reasons for those feelings and for the audience behavior."

I had delivered the above statements in a flat, declarative voice devoid of humor or warmth. This was early in a communications workshop and these people didn't know me very well yet. The audience was silent and Jack (my questioner) was looking down at a pad on the table before him. "Jack," I began again, "I notice that you've fallen silent, would you care to share with the rest of us what is going on with you at this point?"

Jack appeared to be surprised and said, "I'm sorry, I guess I was thinking about what you said and about that awful session I had that led to my asking the question."

I then said, "Jack, could you have also in any way been turned off by the word "M'lad" and by the rather superior tone I used in replying to you?"

This time Jack was surprised afresh, but also appeared rather uncomfortable. "No—no—," he stammered, "I guess I didn't notice."

"I was, " Larry, a companion of Jack's said, "it sounded like you were talking down to him."

"I was, in a rather gentle way, but it was a kind of parent to child transaction." I then asked if any of the others had reacted negatively to my response and found that about one person out of five had taken notice of, or exception to, the way I answered Jack. I then asked several more participants what had been going on with them at that time. Most said they were thinking about what I had said or were thinking about something else—often a personal experience they had had with an unresponsive audience. By now the exchange was becoming more lively. I then said:

"This discussion, I think, illustrates my principal points about dealing with an unresponsive audience."

1. *The audience has reacted*—even if by thinking, becoming preoccupied with their own thoughts, being turned off, or not considering the subject significant enough to worry about.

2. *There are reasons for that reaction*—they are in some way reacting to their own needs or dealing with their own feelings. These reasons may or may not have anything to do with you.

3. *Different people have different thresholds for negative responses.* My treatment of Jack apparently didn't bother him because of his preoccupation, though it annoyed some (though not all) of his associates.

4. *You often need their help* in overcoming problems that are causing a group to be unresponsive.

By starting this discussion and listing these four points on a newsprint pad, I illustrated an important way to deal with a nonresponsive audience.

AUDIENCE MOOD

If we aren't getting much from our audience there are reasons, which make sense to them.

"No emotion" is often a hiding or cutting off of feelings. Coldness often means suppression of feelings, while an icy stare may reflect anger. Although we can't always be sure we are reading these signs accurately—this may be all we have to go on. However, if we can perceive even something of what our listeners are experiencing we have a chance to do something meaningful to them and engage their interest.

If the group problem is boredom, be especially alert. Boredom can drain energy, but for many people it can also be a precursor of action, and often not the action you want. Our creative subconscious mind often generates more interesting things for us to do that may be perceived by others as troublesome.

Often the person who does seemingly stupid or dysfunctional things when bored isn't even aware of why they did what they did. If boredom is an issue, we need more interesting activities, even if some of our content is lost. Consider whether covering your material or achieving your goals is more important. I have seen many speakers trudge through their planned presentation even when the snoring was deafening.

Our challenge is to find something interesting for them to do even if it is only to socialize for a few minutes before returning to the subject of the meeting. Boredom can be fleeting. Once we spark their imagination they will often fan the ember into a flame.

Despair is a special problem and comes in many forms. The group that feels that "they must listen to a speaker regardless," feels defeated. The sadness of "having" to spend a portion of their life on something they don't want to do can be very debilitating and can lead to anger. When people believe that their viewpoint won't be considered, their feelings will be disregarded and they will not be able to affect the outcome of the meeting or any consequent action that may result, they feel hopeless and helpless.

THE LISTENERS CONTROL THEIR FEELINGS

What are their needs and interests? Has the group been numbed by previous boring sessions? Are they being punished? Do they have some negative misperceptions about the other people at the meeting? Are they fearful, and if so, about what? Are they punishing you or someone else? Whatever the source of their condition, you are dependent upon them to solve it.

Because we overlook the fact that the other person's feelings are generated by them and within them, we often indulge in magical thinking and believe that we made a group laugh or cry or jump up and shout. In reality they always determine their response.

Sometimes it becomes a contest as to who will control how they feel, and they hold the high ground. If they are angry at you or at the person or organization that you represent, they may decide to punish you by not laughing at your jokes or rejecting your overtures. In this case we generally have five main courses of action:

1. You can try to clarify the problem and listen (with reflective feedback) to their concerns.
2. You can confront them with the problem and ask for their help.
3. You can act enthusiastic and try to transmit some enthusiasm to them.
4. You can appeal to their imaginations, especially through the use of humor.
5. You can involve them in activities that provide an opportunity for them to change their mood.

Problem Clarification and Listening

A colleague of mine was hired as an after dinner speaker, to give a talk to a group of banking managers and executives and their wives. When he arrived the tension was so thick you could slice it. There was virtually no small talk and their eyes were riveted on the speaker as people sat tensely waiting. He wanted to probe their obvious anxiety before he began his talk. He asked both wives and husbands to choose one word that described how they personally were feeling and to say that word aloud. The responses began with expressions such as "okay," and "so, so," but became more bold and definite as he solicted more responses. The responses began to range everywhere from "tense" to "sick" and from "scared" to "angry."

He asked what caused those feelings and discovered that at a company banquet a couple of weeks before, they had been told that they were to have a session with a psychologist, that they "were to bring their wives" and that "they had better show up."

Faced with these effects of that clumsy meeting announcement the presenter listened out their concerns, acknowledged them, and then explained that he had no intention of putting anyone on the spot. He said he simply wanted to share some ideas with them about interpersonal communication that he thought would be helpful to them in their personal lives and in their business relationships. He also said he hoped that they would be comfortable sharing some of their thoughts with other people in the group and to think about this experience when the session was over. He knew that once they had chosen that one word— which defined themselves at that moment, and had spoken it, they would no longer be a totally cold or uptight group. He was right—they became very involved and talkative once the ice was broken. If the emotions of a group can be brought out effectively, tension usually drops.

Confrontation

A friend of mine was assigned to talk about a managerial method called Management by Objectives (MBO) to a group of administrators at a university. The group was more than bored, it was lethargic, uninterested, and despondent. The speaker confronted the group and solicited their view. They said that MBO had been tried before and hadn't worked and they did not believe that they could set measurable objectives in an educational institution but "just knew they were going to have to put up with it again."

The speaker expressed his appreciation for sharing their feelings. Then he said he thought that there was some merit in MBO and would appreciate it if they'd listen to them for thirty minutes and then they would do an exercise that he thought they'd find interesting. By the end of the day they were writing measurable objectives for some areas of their jobs and were enthusiastic about their expanded capabilities. If we can identify group feelings and their cause, we can often confront their behavior and develop plans for dealing with them.

Whipping Up Enthusiasm

Some "stump" speakers are dynamic enough to convey some of their energy to their audience. Others are able to manage words well enough and ignite their listeners' interest. Some can do both. When we watch such a person perform we may assume that these abilities are a natural talent or part of their innate personality. In some cases perhaps they are, but someone who seems to lack these gifts need not despair nor leave the field to others.

The relaxation techniques discussed earlier can generate energy and facilitate your flow of words. As we have suggested, an imaginative, well-crafted presentation can use a variety of audio and visual techniques to arouse and captivate an audience so that they supplement and accentuate your natural talents. Lastly, a well-written speech which takes into account such things as the rhythm and cadence of your words can produce surprisingly good results. A lack of natural ease can be compensated for if we carefully use what talents we have to rouse our audience.

Can We "Make" Them Laugh?

If you've ever succeeded in getting someone to laugh "in spite of themselves," you know that there are ways to get through to people if only we can find the way. While finding the way is *our* challenge, they already have in place the very thing we need to get them going, and that is their creative subconscious mind.

They may have made up their mind that "they aren't going to give you the time of day," and as long as you keep asking for it, you aren't likely to get it. However, if you ask when this session is supposed to be over, they will probably tell you. Then if ten minutes later you ask how long before the session is over, probably a dozen people will tell you, without realizing that they had just given you the time of day.

In a similar way we can't *make* people laugh—they may decide not to. However, with humor we have something going for us that seems almost magical. There is an almost involuntary part of us that decides to laugh when certain kinds of events occur. This is the spontaneous reaction to our emotions. The mechanism is the same as with all basic emotions such as joy, fear, grief or anger that are triggered by how we perceive an event. So with humor we "might" be able to evoke an *instantaneous*, *unthinking* response from a person's subconscious mind.

Humor often results from pursuing a certain logical path and then giving out an incongruous statement that cuts across all aspects of the logic. This switch releases tension, causes laughter, and changes the mood sometimes, in spite of a person's conscious desires. The grappling iron, however, that enables all of us to grasp humor is the problem that the story or joke poses for our imagination. The problem operates on both conscious and subconscious levels. For example:

The pilot of a small commuter airplane that was 40,000 feet in the air came on the radio to announce to the four passengers: "Gentlemen, I've discovered a fuel leak that will cause us to run out of gasoline. We can't make a field. The plane is on automatic pilot but it is going to crash and we have only four parachutes for the five of us. Now, since I'm the pilot responsible for this flight and have to fill out a report on the crash and attend a lot of government hearings to explain this disaster, I think that I should get a parachute."

After talking it over the others agreed and the pilot bailed out. Another man rose to say that he was the President of the United States and that he had a mandate from the people and that over 200 million people were expecting him to carry out that mandate, therefore he thought he should have a parachute. After talking it over, the others agreed and the President bailed out.

Then another man rose and said: "I'm . . . and I've won four Nobel prizes in different fields. I'm reported to be the smartest man on earth and my continued contribution to humanity is so great that I think I'm entitled to a parachute." The other two agreed and the smartest man on earth bailed out."

Left were a priest and a hippy. The priest said: "Since my business is up there and your business is down there, you take the parachute."

"Don't worry about a thing, father," the hippy said, "the smartest man on earth just bailed out wearing my backpack."

When the punch line is reached, there is a general release of tension and people laugh. They become absorbed with the progressive logic of the story and when the incongruity is revealed it tickles their imagination and laughter results. In most jokes listeners are presented with a dilemma that demands their immediate attention—a plane is crashing, and only four parachutes are available for five people. The plot is gradually developed, through the pilot's, the President's, and the scientist's reasoning, to involve the listeners fully in the story and make them eager for the outcome. When the priest and the hippy are left, the listeners can't help but expect the wrong conclusion. If the joke is told well, the punch line takes them by surprise. The conclusion is ironic and people laugh. All of the lead-in is necessary to provoke the intended response—spontaneous laughter.

It is the nonlogical side of all of us, our spontaneous, creative and imaginative side, that helps a speaker make contact with a distracted or turned off person, even when humor is not involved. Almost anything that stimulates, excites, intrigues or challenges them is likely to do the trick. Tickle their fancy and you have begun the march toward your objectives.

However, this point on control is important. When we tell a joke and arrive at the punch line, we provide the critical event, but their perception of the event triggers the laughter. Thus in a strict sense we don't "make them laugh," we provide the opportunity to laugh, an opportunity that most folks are quite willing to jump for spontaneously since it feels so good. This is such a quick reaction that the person often doesn't have time to consciously think it through. If they do take the time to think it through, the laughter will be delayed. If they think too much about it, the joke may die a lingering death. This is why when a joke is explained, it loses its humor and effect.

However, since it is their perception that triggers the laughter, based on the almost instantaneous association and contradiction, their mind meshes with other things they know and they make themselves laugh. This inner control over laughter explains why some people "don't get the joke," because the proper associations with the absurdity are not available to their mind. This inner subconscious control also explains why, when we are spoofing a group and we suddenly reveal the spoof, most of the group may laugh but a few may become offended or angry. If the subject turns out to be risque some may smile "in spite of themselves." That is, their imagination has overriden (parental) messages they have about what is proper and what is not.

From a speaker's point of view there is no need to criticize ourselves if we do not "make people laugh" or "get through to them." The energy expended in such negative self-appraisal might better be spent designing better ways to reach out and touch their imagination in the next situation.

Activites that Change Moods

How do you get a nonresponsive group to develop interest and involvement in your agenda? Three possible answers are: Icebreakers, Blockbusters and Shock Treatment.

Icebreakers   If a group lacks energy, the issue for a speaker is: how can I get them involved? Energy levels can change substantially with interest level. You know how tired you've been sometimes and someone suggested an activity that you love and you suddenly become a human dynamo—often it is so with groups.

People usually love to talk about themselves and sometimes like to find out about other people. When starting to work with groups of up to about 30 people I often ask them to work in pairs with someone they don't know and learn some things about the other person that they can tell the whole group by way of introducing that person. Most people turn to the task with enthusiasm.

Small group discussions, of a question of interest to the participants, can get people feeling more comfortable and interchanging freely. There are also more personal and subtle ways. A man I worked for once brought a bag of peanuts to a meeting. As he began to talk informally to the group, which was very reserved, he began to shell the peanuts and eat them. Some group members were surprised while others were puzzled or offended. Gradually, however, he began to toss some peanuts to people seated near him. Some responded by eating them. Gradually his peanut partners grew in number and then he made his point: "Isn't it better when we all participate?" That was the theme of his presentation and I doubt if anyone there has ever forgotten the peanut experience. You may prefer other approaches, but think of your theme first and then of informal, comfortable ways to introduce it.

Blockbusters   Unless passivity based on hostility is at a high level, most audiences will cooperate with requests from the speaker, unless the request is seen as too threatening. Also, when people have uncertain or negative feelings they sit as close as possible to people like themselves or people they know. They also seat themselves as far from the speaker as they can get. How do we break up these blocks or groupings or create new groupings to stimulate interaction?

The layout of the room is important. If the people are sitting theater style, very small groups of three or four can discuss an issue or share viewpoints, even pairs is satisfactory, and if you ask them to talk with someone they don't know, most of them usually will.

When people are formed around a "U," you can go around the "U" and quickly count them off one, two, three, etc., for the total number of groups that you want and then say: All the "one's" over here, the "two's" over there, etc. Though some confusion may result, they usually sort it out and are now working in groups where their close friends are few.

If the people are at rows of tables facing the presenter, I often ask a segment of the first row (two or three people) to turn around and work with those behind them. This method of forming groups is often a fast and effective way to get people talking to those they don't know.

Trainers and group–work specialists have a lot of ways to break up natural social groupings if such groupings are encouraging passivity or resistance. Whether a speaker is able to redistribute social relationships during a meeting or whether this is desirable is often a matter of the speaker's judgment.

Shock Treatment   This type of powerful, but often touchy approach to changing audience mood takes a great deal of judgment and skill. Planting people in the audience to stir up debate, gimmicks and games and outright audience shockers virtually guarantees that an audience will change—but not always for the better. One politician brought a starter's pistol to a meeting and said with a broad smile, "I've heard that this was a tough audience, so I came prepared!" He then fired the pistol into the air only to find that a woman in the front row fainted dead away—an event that certainly stole the spotlight from the speaker.

Some speakers prefer almost any change in an audience's mood and will use any device they can find to effect a change. Other speakers prefer to merely work up their own level of interest with the expectation that the audience will catch fire as their enthusiasm waxes. Often these methods work. The speaker may be very successful in "playing" the audience successfully. But this often takes a lot of energy and a finely tuned sense of what is of interest to that particular group. However, there is a way to get to at least some people in every unresponsive group. Often it is a matter of expanding your repertoire of techniques and honing those to a fine edge.

CHAPTER NINETEEN

Managing
special situations
and special problems

As the tear gas canister rolled down the isle and people scrambled to get out of the hall, Elisha Throckmorton Quirksburry, fearless international negotiator and speaker extraordinary, dabbed a tear from his eye as he stood at the podium and said:

"So this is going to be another one of those days, huh?"

For a speaker courageous enough to undertake dealing with known difficult or hostile audiences, it may seem as though every day is one of those days. Though we have discussed how to prevent audience problems, how to overcome challenges that do arise and how to make our presentation more effective, there are still at least six problems or situations that merit special attention. These are:

1. The irretrievable blooper.
2. Handling organized opposition.
3. Recovering a disrupted meeting.
4. The gratuitous speech or remark from the floor.
5. The hostile interview.
6. The hostile press conference.

There are no simple answers, to any of these situations. However, by sharing some thoughts and information, perhaps you'll be better prepared when the going gets rough.

THE IRRETRIEVABLE BLOOPER

The candidate's motorcade was running late—he had been zig-zagging all over a large part of the Mid-west. He rushed into the high school auditorium in a small community, swept onto the stage, was introduced briefly by the mayor of this community and began his speech.

"Fellow Americans, it is a great honor and privilege to be allowed to speak to this august assemblage of citizens in Toothbrush, Arkansas."

From the expression on the people's faces he began to realize that he had done it again. Actually, he was in Toothpaste, Kansas, and another politician tasted a bit of dust. The next morning his faux pas was recorded in all the national newspapers.

Where does such a blooper come from? It might be from poor staff work, confusion or exhaustion. In other cases a blooper might spring from the speaker's suppressed hostility or resentment; a lack of personal control or self-discipline; or even from an unfortunate combination of circumstances or words.

It is probably impossible to eliminate all chance of offending or irritating people without missing the opportunities inherent in spontaneous and creative interchanges with an audience. A canned audiovisual presentation is canned, and people know it. Even recorded TV spots have been known to contain errors of judgment, and an experienced speaker reading a carefully prepared speech can stumble over some words with bizarre results.

Yet a platform faux pas is seldom irretrievable and even then some efforts to rescue yourself may be profitable.

For prevention, you can question details in your planning and staff work using Kipling's six honest serving men: "What? Where? Why? When? Who? and How? You can learn to say "No" when becoming overbooked or worn out—some public appearances can be cancelled without the world coming to an end—if you do so early enough. You can anticipate some kinds of negative interactions and mentally rehearse positive outcomes, thereby instilling a subconscious expectation that you'll be able to handle any problem that arises, with equanimity and self-control.

Recognize that the arrow cannot be recalled to the bow; once you've put your foot in it, no amount of lying or fudging is likely to get you out of it. Therefore, basically you can:

- Acknowledge the mistake, apologize and go on with your presentation.
- Say that you misspoke or didn't intend to convey a particular thought or feeling, and try to correct it or the impression that you made.
- Ignore the whole thing and hope that they will too.
- Laugh along with them and then go on with your work.

However, look for clues as to whether or not they are ignoring your error, and respond appropriately if the signs are bad.

In all cases, think before you begin to respond so that you have your ducks in a line and do not compound your error.

HANDLING
ORGANIZED OPPOSITION

Organized opposition implies preplanned collusion rather than spontaneous protest. Whether this had led to organized picketing, demonstrations on the floor, or just an agreement among a few participants to heckle the speaker, such a group generally comes to a meeting with objectives set, scenario in hand and methods worked out for influencing your meeting. Such plans may include total disruption of your meeting, a media event to gain publicity for their cause, or a walkout by a militant or vocal minority.

Few speakers should be caught flat-footed by organized opposition. Most often a group trying to pressure you is easily discernible beforehand and very often their behavior is a logical consequence of the level of organization achieved by those who oppose you. Unless you know little about your audience beforehand or little about their level of agitation, you should project the likelihood of organized opposition and plan for such contingencies. What form your opponent's action will take is often difficult to anticipate, but preliminary intelligence work should help you determine whether they are likely to use strong measures or relatively innocuous protest.

It may be necessary to research your audience for indications that the opposition will be organized and what forms that opposition is likely to take. This can be done right up to the moment of the meeting by soliciting viewpoints and opinions of knowledgeable people, by looking up the history of the group, the kinds of meetings they have generally conducted, where the opposition has come from, and whether it has been spontaneous or planned. Whatever the end result is, you should be reasonably ready with plans laid for counteraction and your resources in place for problems as they arise.

In recent years we have seen the proliferation of single-issue groups such as the Right to Life, welfare mothers, and anti–gun control groups who are focused intensely on achieving one specific set of closely related goals. The power of these groups often rests on their ability to assemble a large and militant group on the steps of city hall or state house on short notice, or to flood a representative's mail with a seemingly universal appeal for a specific action.

The job of the meeting planner or speaker is to maintain your perspective and not be stampeded into hasty or foolish action. You need to assess the true dimensions of this organized advocacy group and the intensity with which they are likely to pursue their ends. Their size and importance need to be appraised against the background of the general population, and the stridency of their advocacy needs to be brought into perspective so that it does not unduly impress you. Their intensity of purpose must be factored into your meeting planning. Thus you can lay plans to neutralize any negative effects they may try to achieve.

None of the foregoing guarantees your ability to deal effectively with all organized opposition, but at least you can reduce the odds or tilt them in your favor.

An important final consideration in choosing your preventative or counter measures is to keep in mind the public image that you want to project or maintain. Overreacting may win the day, but can damage the public view of you and your viewpoint. If you are in any way dependent on other people's good will, either with your audience or with the general public, excessive measures may deny you the support needed to bring your objectives to fruition.

RECOVERING THE DISRUPTED MEETING

Meeting disruptions come in a multitude of forms ranging from bomb threats, power failures, international crises, blizzards, hostage seizures, presidential assassinations, and attempted assassinations, to inter-groups fights, protest marches and attempts to seize the meeting hall. For convenience they can be grouped into two main categories. First, those that are (or perceived to be) external to your group and second, those which are integral to your audience or shared by a substantial portion of the group.

The first category includes shocking or disturbing news, such as the assassination of a public figure, where reports are coming in by television or radio as your meeting progresses. Another type would be an on-going nagging concern where an external crisis develops over several hours or days and uncertainty exists as to what course of action should be taken, as when the snowfall is getting deep and the roads icy or when an international crisis is brewing.

When external events or forces actually intrude upon your group's activities, there is no single "correct" way to respond, except that the safety of the group is paramount. Aside from preplanned scenarios or evacuation procedures built into your earlier planning, a few general guidelines may help.

The group will usually work with you in meeting external challenges if you show a reasonable concern for their needs. For shocking or disturbing news you might offer a brief report on the situation and a recess so that participants can talk over the events. A promise to fill them in on significant developments as they occur may be all that you need to get them back on track. On the other hand, where a nagging concern persists, group efforts to develop acceptable plans for managing emerging crises can help them to settle down. An agreement to dismiss early and to reconvene at another, specific time and place, may allay their fears enough to get some additional work done. Keeping a troubled audience in place is not the goal—achieving your objectives is. If they aren't concentrating on the issues before your meeting, you may be wasting your time anyway. Recovery of a disrupted meeting depends upon their restored involvement, not just their presence.

Where the problem is internal to the group, you may need to apply the problem solving and conflict resolution techniques we've dealt with before to restore group involvement in working on the problem at hand. But here, in addition to showing genuine concern for group needs and concerns, you are more likely to use reflective feedback "I" message confrontation and other interpersonal techniques that cast the intrusion as an opportunity to build improved relationships with the group.

THE GRATUITOUS SPEECH OR REMARKS FROM THE FLOOR

These unwarranted digressions are extraneous contributions offered to further some purpose of the person who is speaking. They are using your meeting as their personal forum. Though there may be an indirect connection with the subject of the meeting, their comments do not further the group purposes.

"Nominating speeches," efforts to sell their own program, product, or concept and rambling monologues that seem to have no point or be leading nowhere; all constitute distractions and usually are an audience irritant, to say nothing of their effects on you as a speaker.

To shut such a person up, confronting their gross behavior, or helping them along to a conclusion without appearing callous or impolite, is quite an art. You might express an audience's concern and let your listeners know that you have their needs in mind, without alienating any of them by letting your interrupter "have it."

To achieve this balancing act you might inform the speaker of the audience's viewpoint, and call upon the group's expressed emotions to back up your statements, such as:

"I can see that many audience members are becoming impatient—could you state your point?"

Some individuals make a regular habit of delivering self-serving or distracting speeches or statements from the floor of a meeting. They will often be playing to a part of the gallery, to their own constituency or to outside observers or the press. Consequently you may need to confront directly using an "I" message such as: "When you take the time of this meeting to expound a cause that is only peripherally related to the issue we are dealing with, your speech consumes valuable time, endangers our objectives and irritates the hell out of me." Note: It helps here to be specific about the speaker's subject and the purpose of the meeting—such as: "You are talking about a candidate for the next election and we are here to discuss differences in fund raising techniques."

Sometimes it is best to let the person run for a few minutes until they get it out of their system, if their behavior is not seriously harming your meeting. If no harm is being done you can thank the person but indicate that "the meeting needs to move briskly along and therefore I'd appreciate it if we could hold off on such statements because of this meeting's time constraints."

Perhaps most important is to stay in control of yourself, to be responsive to the general audience and if possible to confront in such a way that you do not abuse the other person and thereby gain sympathy for them.

THE HOSTILE INTERVIEW

An interview by a hostile reporter means that you may be trying to get beyond that "human filter" to reach the reporter's audience. At least you will be trying to influence the content, the tone, or the viewpoint expressed in their reporting. You can never be sure that your words will be repeated accurately, in context, or fairly. The better reporters generally do report accurately what transpires. But when their mood is hostile or when they become emotionally involved in building a story or when they are biased about the issue, their judgment can be adversely affected. There are a few ground rules that can help guide you in such an encounter, and some techniques of interviewing that it is well to be aware of.

To gain perspective on a potentially difficult interview, remember:

1. The decision to grant an interview is almost always yours—you do not

have to be interviewed. If the cards are, or could be, stacked against you, you may well consider not participating.

2. You often have the right of termination and may do so, if the interview is not serving your purposes.

3. You often do not have to respond to questions nor do you have to answer them, and you can frequently divert the question to talk about things that are of value to you.

I am not suggesting an adversarial role, simply that this is your interview and unless you are directed by higher authority to participate, you may respond any way you choose.

There are consequences to any response you make or even if you don't respond at all. A reporter always has the last word and can state that "the speaker terminated the interview in a huff." It might be better if he or she had to report only that ". . . was unavailable for comment." This ability of an interviewer to *interpret* your response and to insert subjective editorial comments creates a hazard for any interviewee.

When your interviewer is hostile it is important for you to know what you want out of the interview and to have a good idea of how you are going to get there. Though the interviewer usually chooses and directs the questions that you are to answer, your responses are only as controlled as you allow them to be.

A brief study of interviewing techniques and of your options will show that you can often manage the interview without getting off the track, dodging issues or twisting the interviewer's questions out of recognizable shape.

1. The *primary* question that opens up a major area of the discussion. These are relatively few in most interviews and usually start with an open-ended question—one that leaves you free to answer as fully as you choose and in whatever manner you wish. When you answer a primary question in a hostile presence, be sure that you reveal what you want to reveal and that you stake out the territory that you consider relevant and useful.

2. *Secondary questions* follow up on comments you made to a primary question or deal with specific points that the interviewers want to pursue. These are often *closed questions* in that they limit the way in

which you can answer, such as with a "bipolar" question that begs for a "yes" or "no" or "good" or "bad" response.

When you are being interviewed on a one-to-one basis, the interviewer frequently begins with an "open-ended question," and then moves to a series of "closed-ended questions." For instance, an open-ended question would be: "Tell us what happened down at the boiler works today." A closed-ended question would require rather specific answers such as: "Was this accident caused by worker negligence or not?" Thus they move from the general to the specific.

In a hostile interview the primary or general (open) questions often represent a morass where you can lose yourself and sink out of sight. Secondary, and often closed questions are the ones that they can use to cut you up into small pieces if you are not careful. These words are not an attempt to make you overanxious, just careful.

Finally, good reporters and effective interviewers are trained to solicit information through *neutral* questions which are not shaded, biased or directed, and which encourage an outpouring of information from the speaker. Where no threat is apparent, but your subject is controversial, beware of disguised hostility. Try to discover any interview bias, perhaps *by asking them* some questions. Check the past writings or viewpoints of your interviewer if you possibly can. Often a biased questioner will expose his or her lack of interest in objective reporting through the use of either leading or emotionally loaded questions, but don't count on such bias being visible. An interview, even when it is hostile, can be a great opportunity; we each must make sure that it does not become a trap.

HANDLING THE HOSTILE PRESS CONFERENCE

Managing the hostile press conference is perhaps one of the most difficult trials that a spokesperson can face. There are several tools and techniques used by people who have to deal with a press conference, whether they be regular spokespersons or someone catapulted by a crisis or extraordinary circumstances to explain events, defend a position or justify a policy.

- Clarify your own objectives and viewpoints.
- Prepare your scenario beforehand, work it out to achieve your objectives.
- Do your homework and stick to the facts as you know them.
- Consider reading a carefully prepared statement—one where you control the information and the output of that information.
- Consider the issue of control, that is, requiring the questions to be submitted beforehand.
- Use the "no comment" approach when you feel it serves your purposes and the alternative could get you into trouble.
- Don't go over old ground that you've covered before, they might catch you in a contradiction or an error. Say simply "We've been over that before."
- Don't be afraid to use the old expression "We'll have to check on that and get back to you."
- Consider admitting it when you don't know the answer or state clearly that the answer is in another person's area of expertise.
- Avoid psychological games—don't let them get you rattled or get your goat. Take deep breaths and relax and respond from a thinking position rather than from an emotional position.
- Don't let them cast you as the bad guy. Confront their ploys—possibly even talk about their behavior and their bias or prejudice. Do this carefully, but do it if necessary.
- Cut off the interview when it has served your purpose. Use the excuse that you're running out of time if you need to cut it off without getting them angry.
- Use the "One more question" routine as a way of signaling that the conference is at an end.
- Don't overtalk, it is often the "throw away" comment that gets you in trouble.
- Finally, the most important item—avoid extemporaneous responses unless you are very good at them.

Overall, a press conference of any type can be used by you for positive ends to meet your own goals and objectives. Often we're required to deal with a press conference when we face adversity but there are usually ways, even then, to turn it around and move toward your own objectives.

It frequently requires a good deal of art, imagination and flexibility to deal with these special problems successfully. It also requires great understanding of yourself and others. But fundamentally you have to believe that with proper planning, practice and self-mastery you can manage anything that is thrown at you.

CHAPTER TWENTY

Managing yourself in the heat of battle

Acquitting yourself well during a hot exchange may be tough, yet rewarding. But when under attack, your "natural" reaction may be to "let them have it," "repel all borders," to "counterattack," to "win out" to "beat them" rather than to achieve your objectives. You may get so involved in the fight that you lose sight of where you are going. The "I showed him" syndrome may get in the way of being effective or of really winning the war.

An effective speaker needs flexibility coupled with an ability to avoid psychological traps where our emotions overpower our thinking process, and a relaxed state of stress inoculation.

AVOIDING PSYCHOLOGICAL GAMES

We have all seen good speakers pulled down because someone in the audience uncovered and pushed a negative "emotional trigger" that set the speaker off, so that they became trapped in inappropriate or excessive behaviors. This is because the speaker was sucked into a *psychological game* and was damaged by the results.

Psychological games are transactions between people based primarily on emotion and habits and consequently they tend to be subconscious, spontaneous, "unthinking," and unaware reactions to events that excite, frighten, anger, sadden or upset us. Participation in such games is not based on logic or plan or even on conscious thought. I might consciously attempt to goad you into an automatic unthinking emotional response and you may bite. However, I'm playing an intentional "conscious" game while you are responding out of anger and in an automatic subconscious (unaware) game mode. Some people will consciously attempt to play on your subconscious. They'll attack you where you're most sensitive, in the hope that you'll respond automatically and emotionally—by flying off the handle or bursting into tears—thereby making a fool of yourself.

Psychological games were originally identified and explained by Dr. Eric Berne in his work on developing a communications model for analyzing basic interpersonal transactions between people (i.e., the basic, verbal and nonverbal messages that we send to each other that become structured in routine predictable patterns). Psychological games are highly repetitive transactions that we tend to play over and over, which produce those familiar negative feelings that we express by such statements as, "Why does this always happen to me?" or, "There I go again!" They are based on negative feelings that we experience when we lock into negative things that our game playing partner is expressing about us.

Psychological games "work" because we have old and often outdated negative feelings about ourselves, other persons, or even about everybody in general. It is often not too difficult to be aware of negative feelings we have about ourselves. All of our inadequacies, past failures and mistakes, give us lots of ammunition for self-criticism, and these negative feelings have often been reinforced by what lots of other folks have said about us since we were young. It is also not difficult to think of individuals or types of individuals that we dislike or have *some* residual anger toward, fear of, or sadness over. Some of us may even admit to having some biases or prejudices over ethnic, racial, religious, or other types of groups. These negative feelings are lodged in our memory along with habitual responses that we express to ourselves or others. When old emotions are triggered, our subconscious produces our old "tried and true" reactions so that we respond quickly and automatically.

The danger in such responses, however, is that they are emotional responses from the past and happen so quickly that our mind does not have the time to assess current reality and decide what is best for the "here and now" situation. If you doubt this, think of the many times you have responded quickly in anger and a minute later wished you had kept your big mouth shut.

For the speaker the issue often is: how do I keep my big mouth shut instead of flying off the handle when they get my goat? You may not play "conscious aware" games, but sooner or later everyone gets involved in the kind of *subconscious unaware* games that I'm talking about. When it happens, you most likely won't be aware of it at the moment because you will be reacting emotionally rather than thinking about what is going on. The other party is also not likely to be thinking.

Defensiveness, fear and despair, as well as anger may be emotional triggers that damage a speaker's presentation. To be caught in a psychological game restricts our flexibility because we are responding to the other person or to the group rather than deciding logically and purposefully what we want to do. In a sense they are controlling our behavior.

I once saw a young, competent anthropological researcher, who had been living in a rural Haitian village for three years, mangle his speech to a group of American college presidents because he got sucked into a game. He had been chosen to speak to this group because of the recognition he had achieved in America for the quality of his professional writings and on the recommendation of two of Haiti's top anthropologists. He was attacked, however, by a few audience members on the issue of "how could a white, middle-class English speaking sophisticated American really penetrate the depths of such an alien culture?" The young man apparently was sensitive to this issue and began to respond defensively to their criticism by talking about how he had struggled to overcome these barriers and wandered far from the purpose of his talk. If he had successfully resolved that emotional issue *within himself* previously, he could simply have said, "I speak French and Creole; I've studied with Haitian anthropologists; I've been well-educated in scientific methodologies; my work has been critically praised in academia, and I've been warmly accepted in the village. I don't believe that you have to have lived in the seventeenth century to study and write about seventeenth-century history. I'm here to share my

findings with you; if you'd like me to proceed I'd be happy to do so."
All of the foregoing was accurate. If a member of the audience had
wanted to pursue the credential issue, the young man could have listened, reflected the critic's emotions and perhaps confronted the behavior. Instead, because of his own inner negative feelings, he got sidetracked and gave a defensive disorganized presentation.

Berne has organized and described the structure (the plays) of
many such familiar games and given them names that describe the
nature of, or the "pay off" from, each game. For instance, it is not
difficult to recognize our participation in some of these classic games:

- Yes, but (when someone is giving you advice)
- Kick me (setting yourself up to come out badly in a transaction)
- Uproar (a high-voiced argument or fight)
- Harried (overloading yourself with projects or volunteer work)
- Cornered (getting yourself into such a mess you've got to do something
  ridiculous to get out of it)
- Stupid (doing a dumb thing that you know better than to do)
- If it weren't for you (I could have married so and so or finished my
  education, and so on)
- Ain't it awful (a group collectively complaining about things in general)
- NIGYYSOB (now I've got you, you SOB)
- See what you made me do (often related to sports)
- I'm only trying to help you (aren't I virtuous)
- I told you so (after giving unwanted advice)
- Poor me (I always come out on the short end)
- See how hard I tried (I'm always being disappointed)
- Why does this always happen to me? (Murphy's law)
- Mine is better than yours (I spent more on my car, home, and so forth)
- Let's fight (make damned fools of yourself)

Many of these games are played in a group setting and there is a good
likelihood that there is a "game master" or two in every difficult audience. However, they will be no more aware of their game playing than
you will of yours—they'll see themselves as good and just and in the
process of "doing what is right." However, they'll have an intuitive
grasp of your emotional vulnerabilities and if you aren't careful they'll
"hook" you.

Psychological games are real things that all of us engage in from time to time. Although we might not consciously engage in such transactions, we often do it when our feelings are seized by something another person has said or done that gets us upset. From that moment on we tend to respond emotionally rather than logically, and frequently get deeper and deeper into it.

There are several simple guidelines that you can use to detect and avoid negative psychological games. These are:

- Try to identify and make conscious your psychological vulnerabilities—those things that "get to you."
- Be in touch with your feelings, become conscious of when you *begin* to feel negative about yourself or others.
- When you begin to experience negative feelings, anger, guilt, fear, nervousness or such, ask yourself: "What is going on here?" and "Why do I feel as I am feeling?"
- Try to detect the *discount* or put-down (of yourself or others) in what has been said or done that is giving rise to your negative feelings.
- Be particularly aware when you are feeling like a victim, a persecutor or a rescuer and step out of that role by saying to yourself: "I don't want that role."
- Start thinking of alternatives to the way things are going.
- Give an unexpected response—this will often end the game or divert it.
- Think before talking; think before acting; pause to put your "conscious aware" thinking processes in charge.
- Beware of *absolutes* such as: always, never, every time, and so on. Such absolutes are almost always false and our subconscious, or the subconscious of the audience members, detect and focus on these and begin to argue with their falseness. This often starts the game.

None of these thoughts or responses will guarantee that you will not get "hooked" into a psychological game but with practice you can avoid most of them.

Psychological games are a major obstacle to personal flexibility because once you allow yourself to be sucked into such a negative interchange you tend to play out the game to its almost inevitable negative conclusion. These are not fun games like Monopoly and Chess. These games hurt.

Three short guides that might be put on a card and placed where you can see it when making your presentation might be:

1. When angry, frightened or discouraged, stop to think about what has been said.
2. Identify and confront the "discount" in that transaction.
3. Confront absolutes.

Psychological games have probably laid low more good speakers than any other phenomenon.

No matter what circuitous route you need to follow during a hot exchange with a hostile audience, keep your eye on the target and head for home! These techniques for avoiding negative psychological games can greatly help presenters to better manage themselves during combat with a difficult group.

STRESS INOCULATION

I was driving over the Southwest Freeway in Washington, D.C. at a pretty good speed when I spotted a long iron rod that had fallen off a truck and was bouncing through the air. When I spied it, it was at eye level. My immediate thought was "if that comes through the windshield, I'm dead." However, I knew *without thinking* that if I slowed down slightly, the speed of the car would lessen enough so that this object would drop below my horizon. Without a conscious decision on my part, that's precisely what happened. I heard that piece of angle iron enter the grill of my car. I gradually pulled over to the side and stopped. While I was doing so I heard the piece of metal fall out unto the pavement.

I had only a thin shoulder along the side of the road on which to stop and decided against getting out of the car because of the danger. I watched the temperature indicator to see if the radiator had been punctured. I saw neither vapors nor an increase in the engine temperature, so in a few minutes I drove on.

I was doing what every human being is well-equipped to do in certain emergency situations, and that is, behaving appropriately without conscious thought. Our subconscious has a mechanism for making very quick decisions intuitively and instinctively, which are not thought through (step by step) in a logical procedure. My subconscious mind knew just how much pressure to put on the brake so that that object would fall below the hood of my car, and yet not to apply enough pressure to run the risk of the brakes locking, causing the car to spin out. This was not, as I emphasize, a conscious decision—everything happened too quickly to *think through* that kind of solution.

However, the most interesting thing about the experience was that after I drove off I spent about forty-five minutes getting home, and only when discussing the incident with a friend did it dawn on me that not only did I make an instantaneous decision that turned out to be the correct one, but that I experienced no stress, excitement or fear during, or after the event.

Previously in such a crisis I'd have been trembling, my heart pounding, and I'd be virtually falling to pieces. However, none of that happened and it occurred to me that the calm competence I had experienced was the result of *stress inoculation*.

I had experienced the *accumulated* stress reduction that is the counterpart of the state of general agitation that some people experience when their lives are full of unmanaged stress. The ability to prepare ourselves quickly for unusual action when we are faced with a crisis has been called the "Fight or Flight" response, to indicate its primitive nature and how instinctive it is in each person. However, we can also calm ourselves through quite natural meditative methods and make this tranquility an ongoing way of the life that can keep us largely immune to the negative consequences of stress.

This stress immunity, however, does not mean that we are unable to respond to crisis. It means that our whole mind and body is alert and able to take action quickly and effectively. If we have a clear enough idea of what we are up against, our creative, protective and intuitive subconscious mind organizes our thoughts and actions to produce the best responses that we are capable of at that time. Therefore, it is possible to prepare yourself through daily mental and physical exercises to handle stress without the usual negative physical consequences, or the post event "shakes" that often follow a threatening incident. This last point also illustrates the reason why we need to gain as much positive training and experience as we can so that our subconscious has a lot of good material to work with when it needs to answer a challenge.

Research on meditation and other techniques for managing stress indicates that people who regularly practice relaxation techniques report improvements in their ability to focus their energies productively, concentrate on the job at hand, develop creative ideas and responses, conserve their energies for longer periods of time and avoid being thrown off stride by surprises or adversities.

Not only do regular meditators begin to function more effectively, their bodies and minds respond more efficiently when a crisis is past. Meditators regularly report (and medical evidence supports them) that their blood pressure, pulse and other bodily signs return to normal more quickly after exposure to strain or stress. Their bodies do a quicker and better job of carrying off the powerful chemicals produced by the stress response, once a crisis has passed. These chemicals can be damaging if allowed to linger in the body.

Before this automobile incident I had been meditating regularly for several months and had achieved a level of relaxation, where my subsconsious mind functioned effectively without becoming unduly upset during the incident or afterwards. It is possible to develop a relaxed state of mind, if you care to call it that, in which a person is calm and relaxed in facing almost all situations. When dealing with a hostile audience that kind of stress innoculation can be invaluable. It can be achieved by almost everyone. In that state your intuitive nature works more quickly and effectively so that your decision making is more accurate and virtually instantaneous. You therefore react more flexibly to the realities of the situation.

I mentioned focused awareness earlier, here I'm offering it again for its on-going cumulative value. A valuable side effect develops when people experience this type of relaxation on a regular basis—they become more imaginative and flexible. They are less bound up by extraneous events and less preoccupied with worries and anxieties. They can therefore respond more quickly to the needs of the situation at hand. Meditation, focused awareness and similar techniques restore our energy, release our creativity and help us to solve problems. We can, with practice, inoculate ourselves against stress so that we can become more relaxed, calm, cool, flexible and competent in all aspects of our lives. However, it is when we work with a tough audience that these competencies have some of their greatest payoffs.

Epilogue

An epilogue, as a short addition or concluding section at the end of any literary work, often deals with the future of its characters. In this case you are, or can be, the hero or heroine of this book.

If you use the meditative self-development techniques we've covered and learn increasingly to avoid the unproductive psychological games that all too often trap speakers and audience members, you can enhance your personal strengths. If you can set productive goals and design and make presentations that move the group toward mutually beneficial goal achievement, you can greatly enhance the quality of your meeting outcomes. Lastly, if you can help people to happily resolve conflict, manage their emotions well and solve problems that afflict them, your contribution to society will be substantial.

The competence, skill, and good will with which you face your audience can benefit many in the years to come.

Bibliography

ANDERSON, RONALD H. *Selecting And Developing Media For Instruction.* New York, N.Y.: Van Nostrand Reinhold Company, American Society for Training and Development, 1976.

BENSON, HERBERT. *The Relaxation Response.* New York, N.Y.: AVON Books, a division of The Hearst Corporation, 1976.

BERNE, ERIC. *The Structure and Dynamics of Organizations and Groups.* New York, N.Y.: Grove Press, Inc., 1966.

CARNES, WILLIAM T. *Effective Meetings for Busy People.* New York, N.Y.: McGraw-Hill Book Company, 1980.

DOYLE, MICHAEL and STRAUS, DAVID. *How to Make Meetings Work.* New York, N.Y.: Playboy Paperbacks, 1976.

FLETCHER, LEON. *How to Speak Like a Pro.* New York, N.Y.: Ballantine Books, a division of Random House, Inc., 1983.

FORBESS-GREENE, SUE. *The Encyclopedia of Icebreakers.* San Diego, CA: Applied Skills Press, 1980.

FROST, JOYCE HOCKER and WILMOT, WILLIAM W. *Interpersonal Conflict.* Dubuque, Iowa: Wm. C. Brown Company Publishers, 1978.

GORDON, THOMAS. *Leader Effectiveness Training L.E.T.* Wyden Books, 1977.

HARRIS, THOMAS A. *I'm OK—You're OK*. New York, N.Y.: AVON Books, a division of The Hearst Corporation, 1967.

JAMES, MURIEL and JONGEWARD, DOROTHY. *Born to Win: Transactional Analysis With Gestalt Experiments*. Reading, Massachusetts: Addison-Wesley Publishing Company, 1971.

LA HAYE, TIM and PHILLIPS, BOB. *Anger Is A Choice*. Grand Rapids, Michigan: Zondervan Publishing House, 1982.

LE SHAN, LAWRENCE. *How to Meditate*. New York, N.Y.: Bantam Books, 1974.

LOSONCY, LEWIS E. *Turning People On: How to Be an Encouraging Person*. Englewood Cliffs, N.J.: Prentice-Hall, Inc., 1977.

MCMASTER, MICHAEL and GRINDER, JOHN. *Precision: A New Approach to Communication*. Beverly Hills, California: Precision Models, 1980.

MONTGOMERY, ROBERT L. *A Master Guide to Public Speaking*. New York, N.Y.: Harper & Row, Publishers, 1979.

MURRAY, SHEILA L. *How To Organize And Manage A Seminar*. Englewood Cliffs, N.J.: Prentice-Hall, Inc., A Spectrum Book, 1983.

NEWSTROM, JOHN W. and SCANNELL, EDWARD E. *Games Trainers Play*. New York, N.Y.: McGraw-Hill, Inc., 1980.

NIRENBERG, JESSE S. *Getting Through To People*. Englewood Cliffs, N.J.: Prentice-Hall, Inc. A Reward Book, 1963.

PNEUMAN, ROY W. and BRUEHL, MARGARET E. *Managing Conflict*. Englewood Cliffs, N.J.: Prentice-Hall, Inc., A Spectrum Book, 1982.

ROBERT, HENRY M. *Robert's Rules of Order*. New York, N.Y.: Jove Publications, Inc., 1967.

RUBIN, THEODORE I. *The Angry Book*. New York, N.Y.: Collier Books, A Division of Macmillan Publishing Co., Inc., 1969.

SHEA, GORDON F. *Creative Negotiating*. New York, N.Y.: CBI/Van Nostrand Reinhold Company, Inc., 1983.

SNELL, FRANK. *How to Stand Up and Speak Well in Business*. New York, N.Y.: Cornerstone Library, 1962.

TAVRIS, CAROL. *Anger: The Misunderstood Emotion*. New York, N.Y.: Simon and Schuster, 1982.

Index